Nutritious Meals

Facts About the Mediterranean Diet and 100% Dairy-Free Recipes

Brenda Piatt

Copyright © 2013 Brenda Piatt.
All rights reserved.

Table of Contents

NUTRITIOUS MEALS INTRODUCTION 1
   How the Mediterranean Diet and the Dairy Free Diet are Different 3

SECTION 1: MEDITERRANEAN DIET 6

KEY INGREDIENTS AND RECIPES 11
   Fruits and Vegetables 11
   Beans and Legumes 14
   Fish and Seafood 15
   Olive Oil 16
   Garlic, Oregano, Basil, and Other Herbs 17
   Whole Grains 19
   Cheese and Yogurt 21
   Protein Sources 22

KEY NUTRITIONAL BENEFITS OF THE MEDITERRANEAN DIET 23

HEALTHY MEDITERRANEAN HABITS 25

MEDICAL BENEFITS 29

MEDICAL RESEARCH 32

EXTRA DIETING AND WELLNESS TIPS 35

SECTION 2: DAIRY FREE DIET INTRODUCTION 40

BENEFITS OF DAIRY FREE - WHY PEOPLE CHOOSE DAIRY FREE 42

HOW TO COPE WHEN YOU'RE A DAIRY LOVER, BUT FOR HEALTH REASONS YOU MUST GO DAIRY FREE . 45

SAMPLE 5 DAY DAIRY FREE DIET PLAN 49

KIDS CAN ENJOY DAIRY FREE DIET TOO 52

RECIPES: 53

DAIRY FREE BREAKFAST RECIPES 53
- Applesauce 53
- Buckwheat Walnut Muffins 55
- Pumpkin Spice Muffins 57
- Milk Free Latte 59
- Banana Nut Bread 60
- Basic Pancakes 61
- Orange Banana Berry Pancakes 63
- Breaded Pancakes 65
- Crepes 67
- Hot Cocoa 68
- Granola Bars 69
- Banbergo Smoothie 71
- Banana Blueberry Smoothie 72
- Breakfast Banana Smoothie 73

LUNCH AND SUPPER RECIPES 74
- Pork (or Lamb) Barbecue Sandwiches 74
- Chicken and Fruit Salad 75
- Clam Chowder 77
- Chicken Noodle Soup 79
- Super Easy Vegetable Beef Soup 81
- Cream of Chicken Soup 83
- Potato Soup 84
- Split Pea Soup 85
- Grilled Garlic Shrimp 87
- Beefy Cabbage Casserole 89
- Rack of Lamb 91

Tuna Casserole 93
Mango and Tuna Steaks 95
Chicken Tortilla Soup 98
Salisbury Steak 100
Balsamic Vinegar Chicken 102
Honey Rolled Chicken Kabobs 104
Basic Fried Chicken 106
Coleslaw 108
Cream Corn 110
Mac and Cheese 112
Squash Soup 114
Chicken A La King 116
Lasagna 118
Cabbage Soup 120
"Cheesy" Vegetable Casserole 121
Sweet Potato Soup 124
Chicken and Dumplings 125
Turkey Burgers 127

SNACKS AND DESSERTS 129

Banana Coconut Honey Oat Bars 129
Pumpkin Pie 131
Cheese Popcorn 133
Chocolate Pudding 134
Chocolate Rice Crispy Bars 135
Coconut Flavored Rice Pudding 137
Crunchy Oatmeal Cookies 138
Yellow Cake 140
Fudge 142
Apple Crumb Dessert 143

DAIRY FREE DIET CONCLUSION 145

Nutritious Meals Introduction

Discover how these two easy diets can improve your health, promote weight loss, and introduce you to an exciting array of foods that will keep your taste buds singing. Separate sections explain the benefits of the Mediterranean Diet and the Dairy Free Diet, with tips, recipes and meal planning. Find substitutions for dairy products that you have grown accustomed to. Based on fruits, nuts, vegetables, beans and grains, these diets are still popular in countries situated along the Mediterranean Sea, today.

The Mediterranean Sea borders 23 countries, in addition to being dotted with several islands. The climate of the area is hot and dry, broken up only by a rainy season. The diet of the natives consist of fresh fruits and vegetables, low fat, and red wine. Add to this an active lifestyle in a climate filled with plenty of sunshine, and you have the making of a healthy population. It is believed that by using the natural resources produced in this region, and a regiment of exercise, life is prolonged beyond that of most Western nations. By following the dietary patterns, set forth from this part of the world, the Mediterranean Diet has evolved.

Studies of different types of diets have led researchers to select the Mediterranean Diet as one of the most overall, effective means to improve cardiovascular health. Often used in comparison to Low Calorie and Low Carbohydrate diets, the results keep on proving that the Mediterranean Diet is a winner. Almost every category tested, weight loss, artery circulation, cholesterol readings, and mortality rates, aced high on the test scores in an improved health status.

Although the Mediterranean Diet, that includes a Dairy Free Diet, has been a way of life for residents of the southern part of Italy and much of Greece, for centuries, it wasn't until 1945 that the unique qualities, took notice. An American physician, by the name of Ancel Keys, began to ponder why American middle-aged men were dying of heart disease, while those in Italy, of the same age group, seemed more resistant to cardiovascular problems. Keys was stationed in Italy, during this time, and decided to perform a study on the differences in the two cultural diets. Although his findings were significant, the public took little notice.

By the 1990s, there had been a change in the attitudes of Americans, regarding health and longevity. Terms like low-calorie and low carb diets were taking center stage, in order to create a healthier society. Medical expenses were climbing from obesity, diabetes, cancer, and most of all, heart disease. It was then that Dr. Keys studies on the Mediterranean Diet, began to take notice. Today, the Seven Countries Study, a continuing study of Keys, is regarded as a leading tool in cardiovascular health. Seven countries were asked to participate in a research that compared lifestyles and diet in relationship to strokes and coronary heart disease. The participants were taken from the United States, Northern Europe, Southern Europe, and Japan. An overwhelming majority of healthy individuals were noted in the Mediterranean region.

How the Mediterranean Diet and the Dairy Free Diet are Different

It is believed that the low content of saturated fat and the high volume of monounsaturated fat, plays a large role in the Mediterranean Diet. The Mediterranean region is well known for its growth and production of olives and olive oil. Ironically, Crete, a Greek Island situated in the Mediterranean Sea, has some of the lowest percentages of heart disease in the world. It is on this island that Archeologists have discovered the growth of olive trees as far back as 3500 B.C. There is also a lack of milk products, poultry, meats and sweets in the Mediterranean Diet, but not eliminated entirely. Fresh fruits and vegetables, grains, beans, nuts and seeds are relied upon more heavily than processed foods, cheeses, and eggs.

Think of a triangle that has your basic food groups. The largest part on the bottom should include olive oil, whole wheat grains, vegetables, fruits, beans, nuts, natural herbs and spices. These items should become a part of every meal. The second, and smaller tier of the triangle, should consist of fish and seafood. Preparing a couple of times a week, more if possible, is recommended for getting the required vitamins. The next section of the triangle, holds poultry, eggs, yogurt and milk, less than once a day, perhaps even once a week. At the top and least important, are meat, sweets and milk, which you should try and shy away from as much as possible.

Starting any new diet requires taking a hard look at how you have been leading your life. If you are used to grabbing a fast food meal on your way home, you need to learn how to prepare your own meals at home. There is little nutritional value in fast food and will create a growing waist line. Planning has to be done in order to have the right food stuffs on hand. You might even enjoy making meals ahead of time and freezing for quick meals. Dehydrating fruits and keeping a blender or food processor within easy reach, are other simple changes that you can make, in preparation of your new and healthy lifestyle.

In this eBook, you will find a wide selection of creative dishes that are simple, yet delicious. Flavored muffins, crepes, pancakes and smoothies will pack your morning meal with tons of vitamins and pump up your energy level for the day. Lunches that use soups and salads in exciting new ways, keep you filled, but not bloated, throughout the afternoon. Recipes for dinner will delight your family with meat, chicken, sides and desserts to die for.

Now that you know what these diets are capable of doing, try some foods that were never on your grocery list, in the past, like soy or almond milk, olive oil, coconut oil, figs and legumes. When combined with fresh herbs and spices, you will find that a fast-food burger just doesn't compare.

Section 1: Mediterranean Diet

Every solid weight loss plan requires increased attention on the foods you eat. But the contents of your diet, however healthy, cannot provide wellness if one fails to remember to structure their lifestyle accordingly. If you want to lose weight, finding solid information is the key to this step. That information can help you achieve the best mindset to reach your goals.

If the extremes of modern day fringe diets impose too great a demand upon your palate, it may perhaps be beneficial to look backwards in time for more natural and traditional diet based health solutions.

Whether your objective is to lose weight or eliminate a chronic health condition, more and more people nowadays are turning to the Mediterranean diet as a means to improve their overall wellness. Providing a delectable variety of proteins, vegetables, and favorite recipes dating back thousands of years, a Mediterranean diet is one, which can enable you a healthier lifestyle while still providing delicious meals.

It doesn't just taste delicious; it's good for you too. The Mediterranean diet first came to the attention of the west in the mid 20th century when studies showed that people living in Southern Europe, where most recipes share much in common, not only had much longer life expectancy, but were comparatively free of chronic conditions such as heart attacks and hypertension compared to their northern neighbors.

It was perhaps a bit over-hyped a few decades ago when it was hailed, due to some misinterpreted facts in early studies, as a veritable fountain of longevity based on dietary factors alone. For example, at the time of the initial studies, the majority of Southern Europeans were still engaged in agricultural labor, and with private car ownership as well as public transport (in most areas) hard to come by, the people walked pretty much everywhere they went. Additionally, they didn't take notice of the more favorable work-life balance common in Mediterranean cultures, the early studies failed to report that an active lifestyle was part of the answer to why Southern Europeans lived longer, healthier lives. Despite this, it's a truism that no diet, however salubrious, is going to be of much benefit without an active lifestyle.

Before becoming the global sensation that it is today, the foodstuffs comprising the Mediterranean diet were based more on easy availability than on any profound ancient wisdom known by the region's early inhabitants, although human intervention played a significant role in which crops became dominant.

Unlike less favorable climates, with short growing seasons and a need for food that would last the long winters, both the choice and quantity of foodstuff in the Mediterranean was vastly greater than that found in less naturally blessed environments. Whereas the common people of the north subsisted mostly on bread, preserved meats, and a little cheese, inhabitants of the Mediterranean, with far more choices, naturally made a habit of eating a rich variety of foods.

As befits its namesake sea, the Mediterranean diet is very rich in seafood. The snaking coast lines and many islands meant that nearly all Southern Europeans had access to fresh fish, clams, mussels and calamari on a regular basis while most northerners only experience with seafood came in the form of salted cod from the distant Atlantic that had been marinating over a mule's back for 6 weeks in the summertime on its way inland. So can it really be surprising that most Germans grew to prefer sausage?

Long growing seasons meant that there was always some freshly harvested produce in the local markets, so the inhabitants rarely had to resort to rat-infested stocks of grain like their climatologically challenged neighbors during sub-arctic winters.

History and trade had a hand in it too. Long before Roman times, the Mediterranean was a highway for the various peoples along its rim. Olives, Citrus fruits, grapes, as well as chickpeas and other legumes that comprise the heart of the Mediterranean diet were distributed via these early trade networks, and then mass-produced in industrial fashion on the vast Roman villas that dotted the body of water they, not unjustifiably, called *Mare Nostrum*, or "Our Sea".

Cash crops like Grapes, wool, and flaxseed were primarily exported, while cheap and easy to grow grains and vegetables were made available as the food supply of the armies of agricultural laborers and slaves upon whom the system rested. Obviously, it was in the Roman's interest for this vast labor force to be as well (yet cheaply) fed as possible. The 1000-year period of political and economic union forged by the Roman Empire did much to ensure that most ingredients composing the Mediterranean diet of today were eaten across the whole region thousands of years ago.

The typical Mediterranean diet is made up of over 30%

fats. However, the saturated fat from red meat and heavy animal fats that lead to clogged arteries makes up only 8% of the total, due in large part to the relatively rare consumption of red meat and preference towards olive oil as a heating agent. Once again, geography plays a role. With most of the farmland along the Mediterranean crowded into fertile valley nestled between mountains or deserts, livestock was mostly used for dairy purposes. Indeed, before Southern European diets were influenced by modern habits, lamb was just about the only red meat consumed, and even then only sparingly, as wool was the main source of clothing.

This diet is not typical of all Mediterranean cuisine. In Northern Italy, for example, lard and butter are the usual heating agents for in cooking, and olive oil is used only for dressing salads and vegetables. In North Africa wine is religiously avoided by most of the locals.

Even though the diets of Southern European's themselves are steadily broadening, the health benefits of limiting your meal's ingredients to those traditionally found along the Med will provide long term benefits and provide a richness of flavor rarely found in the "fad" diets promoted by one weight loss guru or the next.

Key Ingredients and Recipes

As computer programmers like to say about code, "Garbage in, Garbage out", the same goes for the ingredients we put into our meals. The first step in using the Mediterranean diet to increase your health is to first learn of what it's composed of, and then using those ingredients in your daily meals.

Fruits and Vegetables

The Mediterranean region has volcanic soils and a 12-month growing season, so it is not surprising that the people of that area, on average, consume nine portions of fruits and vegetables every day. Mediterranean residents generally purchase their produce from farmers markets and produce stands. They also enjoy it when it's most flavorful by consuming "in season" produce.

Vegetables provide the most antioxidants needed for health and longevity when they are heated and processed only minimally. Even more important, the variety of vegetables and fruits commonly consumed gives people who have trouble sticking to diets a higher chance of success due to the greater choices available.

In Addition to Mediterranean fruits and vegetables now consumed globally like oranges, grapes, and lemons, some of the key Mediterranean fruits and vegetables are:

Artichokes

Renowned for their flavor since ancient times, artichokes are in fact flower buds from a type of thistle plant. It is not advisable to eat artichokes raw, since only a small part of each bud is edible. In fact, prepping raw artichokes takes even an experienced chef a great deal of time. When cooked, however the tender bottoms on the inside of the bud's and the middle of the plant called the artichoke "heart" taste utterly divine. If you purchase raw artichokes (which are usually much cheaper due to the amount of effort it takes to prepare them for cooking), avoid those with leaves that point away from the middle of the plant center, because they will be mostly inedible fiber. If you wish to savor a traditional artichoke recipe, bake some with butter. Sprinkle some olive oil and vinegar over the finished artichokes and enjoy. Of course, if you want a quick snack, pre-cooked artichokes can be substituted. They are commonly available in cans or jars at most supermarkets.

Figs

A favorite across the entire Mediterranean region, the fig is a sweet fruit grown on the *Ficus carica* (fig tree). The Fig tree is a native to the Middle East but grows very well in the Mediterranean climate. Figs contain many antioxidants and are a good source of flavonoids and polyphenols. They are one of the highest plant sources of fiber and calcium, which promotes strong healthy bones.

Fresh figs do not have a very long shelf life. You will probably find dried figs or fig preserves more easily. If you are fortunate to find fresh figs try the ancient delicacy of dipping them in honey, or you might enjoy drizzling a little chocolate on them for a real burst of flavors.

Eggplants

Most Europeans know Eggplant as Aubergine. It is widely consumed cooked in savory dishes. Mistakenly it is referred to as a vegetable when if fact it is a fruit.

Eggplant is very popular in Mediterranean cuisine. The people of Lebanon and Israel grill the eggplant and then combine it with tahini, lemon juice, garlic and a bit of salt to make a dip called Baba Ganouj. It is served with warm pita. It is a key ingredient in Ratatouille, a vegetable relish with tomato, garlic, zucchini, onion and herbs from Southern France. And the delicious Greek Moussaka would just not be possible without eggplant.

Most Mediterranean eggplant has bitter juices that must be drained off before the eggplant is cooked. The best way to do this is simply sprinkle slices of eggplant with salt and let it sit for a while. The juices will be drawn off and the flesh will then be delicious.

Beans and Legumes

While many of the beans and legumes found in the Mediterranean diet were, like potatoes, brought from across the Atlantic during the 15th century, other has been a feature for thousands of Years. Black and red beans figure prominently in Spanish Cuisine. Fava Beans, Kidney beans, and lima beans as commonly featured in regional dishes as well. Chickpeas are featured prominently, being the basis of many stews in the Western Mediterranean, like Spanish *garbanzo* soup and in the east it is mixed with Tahini to produce delicious humus, a staple food, especially favored in the eastern Mediterranean and the North African coast.

A Typical Mediterranean inspired salad could be made with leafy greens. Include some tomatoes, peppers, carrots, onions, beets and radishes and drizzle a little vinegar and olive oil on top. Make roasted vegetables like peppers and eggplant a regular addition to your diet. Gain maximum health benefits by striking meat from the menu two days a week. Meat is not the only source for protein. You can get plenty of good protein from beans and lentils.

Fish and Seafood

American grocery stores usually have tiny fish counters and enormous meat counters. This is right in line with the typical American diet that includes copious amounts of red meat and little seafood.

Seafood and fish should be more prominent in your diet. They are low in calories and high in omega-3 fatty acids.

Southern European diets, going all the way back to Julius Caesar's time, are high in mussels and clams, octopus, squid and other seafood. Of course most people of Southern Europe live within 20 miles of the sea. So they have ample access to these iron rich foods. Northerners on the other hand are land-based and subsequently have diets of more red meats. Simple logistics made this a reality since seafood could not be shipped to far without spoiling.

When selecting the method your seafood is prepared choose sautéed, grilled, steamed and roasted to keep the health benefits. Deep-frying in fat is obviously less healthy.

One example of a healthy alternative to frying would be to mix calamari in with pasta or rice. You could add saffron, mussels and some red peppers to the calamari and rice to make Spanish Paella.

Olive Oil

Saturated fats and hydrogenated oils should sound a loud "stay-clear" signal. A healthy Mediterranean Diet has no place for these two health thieves. The Mediterranean Diet gets some fat from fish and cheese but the majority is from olive oil. Olive Oil is very popular in the Mediterranean region. Grazing land is a premium and olive trees flourish. Each tree is capable of producing several gallons of oil per season. Olive oil is a wonderful dressing for salads, makes a good butter replacement on bread and offers many health benefits. It has been reported that olive oil can lower LDL (bad cholesterol) levels and is a good source of antioxidants. Both can reduce the risk of heart attack.

Garlic, Oregano, Basil, and Other Herbs

Many Mediterranean dishes include garlic, which is well known for its marvelous health benefits. Some benefits associated with garlic are:

- High in antioxidant compounds which promotes a healthy heart and immune system.
- Has germanium, which is an anti-cancer agent. Garlic has more germanium than any other herb.
- Lowers blood pressure, serum triglycerides, and LDL – cholesterol and prevents arteriosclerosis reducing the risk of heart attack and stroke.
- Improves joint health. Studies show garlic eaters were less likely to suffer osteoarthritis.
- You can increase your consumption of garlic by infusing it into the oils you cook with or adding some to the water you boil your pasta in.

For additional flavor boosts use spices like basil and oregano. You will add flavor to your food without increasing sodium in your diet.

Acetate, Borneol, Bisabolene, Carvacrol, Caryophyllene, Cymene, Geranyl, Linalool, Linalyl Acetate, Pinene, Terpinene and Thymol are all in the oils and leaves of Oregano and Basil, making both sources of internal and topical health benefits.

Basil is high in the essential mineral magnesium, which improves blood flow by relaxing blood vessels.

Many have found that eating basil regularly helps digestion. Studies have shown basil has strong antibacterial properties. These components battle parasites in the colon and intestines, as well as fight off some bacteria that are resistant to modern antibiotics.

Basil oil is a good remedy for stomach problems like indigestion, cramps and constipation. It is also effective at treating colds, flue and sinus infections. Studies show that it may help treat whooping cough, bronchitis and asthma.

With basils many health benefits you would do well always have some on hand. There really is no reason you can't, as it is one of the easiest herbs to grow. All you need is a sunny spot in the kitchen and a pot large enough to grow healthy roots.

Adding basil to your diet is easy, it is the primary ingredient in pesto sauce. For A tasty pesto sauce boil 2 parts spinach with 1 part basil add some ground pine nuts and olive oil and salt to taste.

Another way to add basil to your diet is to simply toss a few leaves into your favorite dish.

One more tip is to add basil oil to your salad dressing; the antibacterial components will fight bacteria on your vegetables and make them safer to eat.

Dry and fresh herbs add burst of flavor and amazing health benefits at the same time.

Whole Grains

When people think of the Mediterranean they think of bread, rice and pasta. Cheese and olive oil seasoned bread is a lunchtime staple. In Eastern Mediterranean regions flatbreads and pita are the standard. Wholegrain versions of these unleavened breads are heaped with nutritional value, all in a compact package.

If you are using the Mediterranean diet as for weight

loss you should limit yourself to whole grain carbohydrates. You can add a bit of flavor with a little Baba Ghanouj, Hummus or simple Olive oil.

Pasta is by an large an Italian favorite, but it is very much acceptable in any Mediterranean diet as long as you are careful to avoid the savory northern Italian recipes which, with their heavy cream sauces, thick lathering of cheese, and use of fatty sausage or meatballs, are mainly designed to fortify a person against the bitterly cold winters in north Italy. Further south, pasta is typically served plain, with some seafood like mussels or clams, using garlic and olive oil or pesto sauce as extra flavor.

Just as importantly, bare in kind that much of Southern Europeans' health advantages stem from a relatively more relaxed and social-minded culture. In the United States, for example, people tend to eat rushed lunches, with a mere 30 minutes to move, eat, and hurry back. Often alone. Anyone seen partaking of an alcoholic drink in broad daylight may be frowned upon, even sneered at publicly, doing so in front of work colleges may even result in a long-winded speech from the boss. Southern Europeans will typically enjoy long lunch breaks, typically about 2 hours (In Spain, its followed by the *siesta,* during which the entire country essentially closes for business) with workmates, family or friends with a full bottle or two of drink lubricating the conversation. In short, they eat to ENJOY life rather than merely SUSTAIN it, and work is the MEANS of living rather than the REASON for it!

Cheese and Yogurt

As mentioned earlier, cows were too expensive to raise to be eaten frequently, so what cows there where traditionally employed producing dairy products. Yogurt was the most common, traditionally being easy to make, and lasting unrefrigerated much longer than fresh milk, a valuable feature during the hot summers. It was a common breakfast dish for the Romans, who commonly ate the plain variety with fresh fruits or honey as a flavoring.

Many Mediterranean cheeses such as feta and Brie are softer and less aged than northern counterparts. This is because, without a long, snowy winter, Southern Europeans had less need of food sources that would stay fresh for 4 months. Cheese and yogurt makes a very important nutritional contribution, which will become clear in the next section.

Protein Sources

As part of a well-balanced diet it is important to ingest sufficient levels of healthy protein. Cheeses that are eaten regularly in the Mediterranean diet including feta, mozzarella and goat cheese are all similar in that they contain a lot of protein in each portion. It is important to remember that protein is a crucial part of the growth process for muscle tissue. Since muscle requires much more energy than other cell types, developing more muscle will aid in speeding up your metabolism, intensifying your rate of weight loss. The seafood, beans and legumes described in a previous chapter are another excellent source **of low**-fat protein. Remember that meats like poultry, chicken, pork and Lamb are consumed, but in small portions only about 3 times a week. For example, chicken is traditionally included in rich dishes.

Key Nutritional Benefits of the Mediterranean Diet

Calcium and Magnesium

Residents of the Mediterranean coast consume yogurt and cheese on a regular basis. Both these foodstuffs are sources of the minerals calcium and magnesium. Calcium and magnesium are valuable to maintain healthy bones and are used by your brain and nervous system to transmit instructions throughout the body. Eating a diet rich in protein and healthy fats like the omega-3 in fish and the unsaturated type found in olive oil additionally increases your body's ability to absorb these and other beneficial vitamins and minerals. Followers of The Mediterranean diet ought to maintain a balanced intake of protein and fat, which makes the minerals, found within the cheese more effective.

"Good" Cholesterol Foods and Low Amounts of Saturated Fats

Even though high levels of it are considered quite harmful, Cholesterol is an essential part of the human body. It controls the flow of water and many other essential chemical compounds to each corner of your body. Cholesterol is a primary ingredient that your body transforms into essential hormones like estrogen and testosterone. Having enough of it in your liver allows you to properly process high-fat foods and helps you process vitamins A, D, and E. Including some of the low-fat cheeses favored in the Mediterranean diet will maximize your levels of good cholesterol while keeping the "bad cholesterol levels" low and within tolerable bounds. Many inhabitants of the Mediterranean shore favor cheese made from goat and sheep's milk. Goat and sheep cheese host less saturated fats and feature the primarily monounsaturated fats which promote a healthy heart.

Rich in Essential B Vitamins

Everyone knows that vitamins are important, but those numbered in the B complex group are additionally so. The ingredients of the Mediterranean diet provide a constant stream of B vitamins including niacin, thiamine, B-6 and B-12. These vitamins are the agents that transform the various proteins, fats, and carbs that end up in your belly into useful fuel to be used for developing muscles and energy. Foods featured in the Mediterranean diet such as Chickpeas, lentils, whole grains, and fish are all rich sources of b vitamins.

Healthy Mediterranean Habits

While considered a traditional, economically backwards region for the past few hundred years by their industrialized, rapidly growing northern neighbors, modernity eventually did arrive in countries of the Mediterranean coastline. However, while urban inhabitants have picked up their share of modern habits like driving and vegetating in front of the TV for extended periods, in the countryside and smaller towns, the people continue to live in a way that, in addition to the healthy diet, naturally promotes long and healthy lives. This is contributed to by both economic and cultural factors.

Healthy Mediterranean Habits 1: Get Some Sun

A high proportion of Southern European's still work in agriculture. It is not unusual to come across farms or vineyards that have been run by the same family for a dozen generations or more. The Mediterranean climate, with its hot dry summers and mild, wet winters, means that most regions can grow different crops year-round, so they don't have a 5 month winter break spent hiding from the cold and binge drinking like their northern neighbors do. This abundance of outdoor activity means they are out in the sun a lot, which means their skin produces a very high amount of vitamin D. Interestingly, skin cancer rates are lower among southern Europeans than people living in other sunny locations with similar climates, such as New Zealand. Some studies attribute this to the higher level of pollution in the upper atmosphere that filters out some of the UV radiation, while others attribute it to the fact that the inhabitants of the Mediterranean rim have had thousands of years to grow a genetic tolerance for sunlight.

Whichever is the case, there is no argument that a lot of time spent outdoors which gives your body the chance to produce its own vitamin D has great health benefits.

Healthy Mediterranean Habits 2: Walk wherever you can

Since Southern European towns and villages date *back* to the middle ages and beyond, they are compact and very pedestrian friendly. While many European Mediterranean residents' own cars, they still walk much more than Americans. This isn't just because the towns are smaller, traditionally, the center of social life in Mediterranean towns and villages revolved around the town square, known in various times and places as the agora (Greek), the forum, (Roman), the Plaza (Spanish) and the Piazza (Italian), the town center is where the cafes, local church, government offices, and daily outdoor markets are usually hosted. Even today on any evening, these venerable places swarm with young couples, families, and retired folks enjoying life together.

Mediterranean Habits 3: Social People are Happy, Healthy People

Social links are very strong on Mediterranean culture, commonly valued as much more important than their economic situation. Indeed, unlike the Anglo-Saxon obsession with measuring personal success with wealth, prestige, or position, Southern Europeans commonly measure their level of fulfillment by the quality of their family and social lives.

This is not just true in the countryside, where in the rugged valleys; the entire population is literally related to everyone else. While it is considered normal in certain countries to come home and catch up on work, it is more common along the Mediterranean to leave work and family completely separated (except, of course, in a family farm or business).

While family life is often the centerpiece of social life, people typically "get on" with each other more. In the cafes and squares that dot the region, newly met strangers commonly swap stories and share drinks over a game like dominoes in Spain or lawn bowling in Italy.

The extra quality time with loved ones and friends spent on social and cultural pursuits is revealed through many studies to be an extra contributor to the lower incidences of anxiety, stress, depression, heart disease and depression among southern Europeans.

Even if you don't work on a farm, or it's impossible to do anything in your town without driving, incorporating a "Mediterranean Mindset" is a valuable addition to taking advantages of its cuisine. The extra exercise with keep you fit, and an extra focus on family activities will add incalculable value to your sense of personal fulfillment.

Medical Benefits

The Mediterranean diet food pyramid has little in common with the Western pattern diet. To Summarize, the top of the pyramid is red meat, which is consumed in small amounts a few times a month. Eggs, poultry and fish get served a few times each week. Small portions of yogurt and cheese are consumed regularly. Olives and olive oil are a regular accompaniment to each meal. Just above the Mediterranean diet's base is fruits and vegetables, with nuts and beans included. Pasta, bread, and other grains compose the bottom of the food pyramid. The Mediterranean diet overall is linked to a lower risk of heart disease and high cholesterol. This is due to the amount of healthy fat consumed from olive oil and cheese, and a more fulfilling cultural mindset in which family and social pleasure outranks work in the hierarchy of needs.

While several diets have been noted, the diet offering the strongest evidence of beneficial health effects to include reduced mortality is the Mediterranean diet.

Primarily a plant based diet; the Mediterranean diet has received many accolades for its high intake of dietary fiber and replacing saturated fats with healthy monounsaturated fats.

For decades westerners have been loath to salt and are surprised with the high salt content in the Mediterranean diet. Olives, anchovies, sardines, capers, salted fish roe, salt-cured cheeses are all staples in the Mediterranean diet, as are olive oil based salad dressings. Consider for a moment that our bodies rely on salt and need quite a bit every day. Studies confirm that Southern Europeans are not plagued with the heart problems that other Westerners suffer with. One main reason is that Southern Europeans are not exposed to the levels of saturated fats as Westerners since they consume much less red meat.

If you do switch your diet from the traditional Westerner fare to the healthier Mediterranean diet you would be well advised to limit your salt intake until your body balances out.

Of course diet is only one part of the health benefits of the Mediterranean culture. Add a balanced lifestyle of physical activity and outdoor labor and you complete the picture.

Genetics is a very small influence to the longer life spans of the people of Southern Europe. Mediterranean residents who changed their dietary habits and lifestyle to mirror the less active and fat laden diet of Westerners were found to have significantly increased their incidence of heart disease.

There is considerable difference in incidence of heart disease in the region between people who stick to traditional foods and those who don't.

The comprehensive benefits of following the Mediterranean diet in relation to good heart health is essentially associative in nature; However they are illustrated in the difference in the geographic frequency of heart disease.

Medical research

While it was known that inhabitants of the Mediterranean enjoyed longer and healthier lives, there was little effort to quantify this until the mid 20th century. One of the first efforts to do so showed that males living on the Island of Crete had a low probability of suffering heart attacks, despite the fact that they ate a substantial amount of fatty foods. In common with other traditional Mediterranean diets, typical meals eaten here include a great deal of olive oil, bread, fresh fruit and vegetables, fish, dairy foods and wine.

Assuming that these low rates were not due to genetics, The Lyon Diet Heart Study included among its goals the aim of showing that any person eating foods found in the Cretan diet could see similar health benefits. The dietary change also required participants to eat much more vitamin C-rich fruit as well as whole-grain breads with a sharp reduction in red meat. Over the multi-year course of this study, the participant's death rate from all causes was reduced by a significant 70%! These results were considered so extraordinary that the supervisory committee decided to stop the study prematurely so that the results of the study could be made available to the public immediately.

This study proved that here were other benefits besides heart health to be enjoyed as a result of including Mediterranean ingredients in a diet plan, inspiring other research teams to quantify other health benefits. A 2008 study of the traditional Mediterranean diet found that if offers a great deal of protection against the development of type 2 diabetes. The study included more than 13 000 college aged students, who did not currently suffer from diabetes, whose eating habits were studied for a 10-year period.

After the ten year study had ended, researchers continued to track some of the participants. It was additionally revealed that who had subsequently continued to include Mediterranean ingredients in their diet had an 80% lower risk of diabetes

A more focused medical study revealed through a UK Medical institute in 2008 proved that persons whose diet is primarily composed of ingredients common in the Mediterranean diet lowered the odds of getting cancer and cardiovascular disease. The results reported a 9%, 9%, and 6% reduction in overall, cardiovascular, and cancer mortality respectively. Additionally a 13% decrease in the odds developing of Parkinson and Alzheimer's diseases was shown as well.

A study published in the same Journal in 2009 shows that some aspects of the Mediterranean diet, including enhanced levels of vegetables without eating a lot of meat is more directly responsible for the overall low risk of mortality than other ingredients, like cereals, dairy, and fish.

Moderate alcohol intake, eating a substantial amount of fruits and nuts, are also associated with lower risk of an early death. Yet another research project published in February 2010 found that eating a mix of Mitterrand ingredients can aid in keeping the brain healthy by reducing the amount of micro strokes that play a large part in the development of senility.

Therefore, in addition to tasting great, offering many delicious ingredients to choose from, and promoting wellness, there is an abundance of scientific evidence proving the efficacy of the Mediterranean diet in reducing risk of a whole slew of chronic diseases. It should therefore be no surprise that the Mediterranean Diet is becoming a comprehensive popular and successful translational paradigm for the promotion of healthier lifestyles.

Extra Dieting and Wellness Tips

The family pet can be an ideal partner in any exercise routine you do alongside the Mediterranean diet. Pets provide unique weight loss motivation and help. You can walk, jog, or just play with your pet. Not only will you and your companion have fun, but also you will be helping yourself eliminate excess body fat from your body.

Instead of consuming sweet snacks every day, go with fruits. If you have been snacking on candy bars, chocolates and other unhealthy items, replacing them with fruits or healthy yet filling Mediterranean snacks like hummus and pita bread provides you with a healthier option with the benefits of the fruits' fiber, vitamins and minerals.

Fostering friendships with those who are fit and healthy can be beneficial to you. These people can serve as models for your desired weight goals. Also, you may be able to pick up extra tips and tricks on how to lose weight.

Make sure to maximize your water intake during the day. If you drink about a half-gallon of water daily for a week and decrease your food intake, you are going to lose water weight. Avoid these strategies, improve your overall diet and increase your activity level for healthy weight loss.

Scan the outer perimeter of the grocery store for healthy foods. Fruits, vegetables, dairy items and meats listed later on in this guide. A little known grocery store fact is those foods in the center aisles tend to be prepackaged, preservative, salt, and sugar-laden and frequently lacking the essential nutrients for a healthy diet. By refraining from walking down these aisles, you will reduce the chance to purchase them.

Track all of the foods you eat and there amounts, as well as your daily activity levels. Studies show that those who keep a journal of these things eventually recognize certain patterns in their habits and find it easier to lose weight. Some people lose a lot more weight just because they pay attention more closely.

A great way to avoid snacking outside of set meal times is to suck on some ice when you're feeling the urge to snack or eat junk food. Sucking on an ice cube can help satisfy a desire to eat.

In order to shed pounds, you must realize the

importance of a proper diet. Go through your kitchen and get rid of all the foods that would interfere with your weight loss, and replace them with traditional Mediterranean ingredients. Eating these healthy foods is the first thing that you have to do in shedding those extra pounds.

Try to avoid wearing lots of loose clothing when losing weight. It is common for overweight people to conceal their weight by wearing loose clothes. You should wear whatever you are comfortable in and not worry about concealing your shape. You are more likely to be cognizant of your weight if you wear clothing that is more form fitting.

Go to bed at a reasonable hour each night. A full eight hours of sleep is the ideal recommendation for adults. If you are thinking that staying up is helping you drop pounds, you are wrong. Getting enough sleep will keep your metabolism functioning properly.

Eating without focusing on portion sizes will lead to weight gain. If you aren't conscious of what you're eating at all times, you may end up consuming much more than you had intended to eat and that will harm your weight loss efforts. Be aware of how much you eat at every meal and you will likely eat less.

Consuming leftovers is a great way to maintain your weight loss regimen. Prepare enough extra portions at your healthy evening meal to take as your lunch the following day. You can make even more to get you through the whole week. This also helps you prepare a quick and simple meal without much fuss the following day.

Many times boredom and thirst can be misinterpreted as hunger pangs. Before you give in to a craving wait 15 minutes. During that 15 minutes drink some water and take a walk. If the hunger pangs persist then eat something.

Almost everyone enjoys the taste of French fries. They are the downfall of many a potential weight loser. Potatoes in general are not heavily featured in the Mediterranean diet, but when they are, they are more commonly heated via boiling or baking, rather than fried in artery-clogging grease. However, if you aren't quite able to quit French-fries altogether, take steps that help erase pounds instead of adding them, like baking them. Slice a small potato into fries, toss with a small amount of olive oil. Then season the slices with rosemary, salt and pepper and bake for thirty minutes in an oven set at 400 degrees. Loosen using a spatula and then bake for about 10 minutes longer. They are great with ketchup and have a much lower fat content, so you won't miss the deep-fried ones.

It is essential that you avoid food that triggers your appetite. This helps a lot of you are in control of your surroundings. You should avoid any contact with trigger foods in your home, your car or at work. If you are exposed to such items often, you may indulge even when not hungry.

Eat your largest meal of the day at lunchtime instead of at night. If you usually have a sandwich during lunch, try having it for dinner instead. You burn far more calories in the daytime and less in the evening, so it makes much more sense to consume more in the daytime and far less at night.

Keeping a healthy weight is the key to your future health. The way you live every day will decide if you can succeed in the long-term. Use what is available to you to make the changes in your life and to create a healthier body. Believe in yourself!

Section 2: Dairy Free Diet Introduction

This Dairy Free Diet recipe book contains over 50 recipes that are 100% dairy free. Some of the recipes are ones you would not expect to find in a book like this like Mac and Cheese, cheesy casseroles, lasagna. There are also breakfast recipes that include muffins, breads, pancakes, and smoothies. You will find lunch recipes of sandwiches and soups and the supper section is the largest with a complete selection of dishes using vegetables, tuna, shrimp, beef, chicken and turkey, plus a few vegan dishes. All the recipes are delicious and fall in lines of a total dairy free diet.

Some of the dessert recipes include Apple Crumb Dessert, Fudge, Yellow Cake, Crunchy Oatmeal Cookies, Coconut Flavored Rice Pudding, Chocolate Pudding, Cheese Popcorn, Pumpkin Pie, Chocolate Rice Crispy Bars, and Banana Coconut Honey Oat Bars. Find recipes here that include cream soups like Cream of Chicken Soup, Potato Soup, and Split Pea Soup. You do not have to go without your favorite creamy foods. There is also a recipe for cream corn here!

Want to fix hearty foods to entertain a crowd? Try the Rack of Lamb, Mango and Tuna Steaks, Honey Rolled Chicken Kabobs, or the Chicken and Dumplings. Want to please children? Try the Chicken Noodle Soup, Basic Fried Chicken, Mac and Cheese, Chicken A La King, "Cheesy" Vegetable Casserole, or the Turkey Burgers. Whatever flavor and style of cooking you like you will find a recipe here to suit your style and flavor. Also included are many family favorites and comfort foods.

Benefits of Dairy Free - Why People Choose Dairy Free

Eating dairy free helps to eliminate the junk foods from the diet. One of the biggest benefits to dairy free is the ability to lose unwanted fat and weight. Today more than ever there is support for engaging in such a diet plan, with many products at the market that are free of dairy ingredients. Eating a dairy free diet along with exercise and drinking plenty of water will help a person to shed the unwanted pounds and fat.

Some of the other benefits of going dairy free are the alleviation of certain physical conditions that tend to be aggravated by dairy foods otherwise. People express feeling less anxious and stressed when they rid dairy from their diets, not only is the stress gone but the energy levels rise. This enables an otherwise sedentary person the energy to get up and do physical activities, which further aids in weight loss. Another good benefit is the help in controlling the cholesterol and blood pressure levels.

Lactose intolerance is a big issue for many adults and the presence of this condition merits going on a dairy free diet. You will find recipes that quickly substitute your favorite dishes less the milk and will be able to eat your favorite foods once again.

Adults are not the only ones who benefit from a dairy free diet children do too. Studies show children with conditions like autism and hyperactivity show improved behavior and reactions when the dairy foods are removed from their diet. Because many of the recipes here are delicious and fun to eat, children on these special diets will not be missing their favorite foods.

Improved health happens a lot while on a diary free diet being the main reason so many is trying it now. Removing dairy foods from the diet helps to control and sometimes even stop certain health conditions. If you have issues that are aggravated by eating milk products, it is worth a try to go a couple of weeks on a dairy free diet. Dairy foods are the cause of more food allergies than most other foods combined. Even moms who breast feed may pass on dairy products to their baby that may exhibit signs of dairy allergies. For those moms it would be wise to try dairy free foods until she weans her baby from breastfeeding. She may find she feels better too without the milk products.

The dairy free diet has other benefits like helping people

to gain muscle mass as it helps to shed fat weight. Normally the benefits of such a diet take a little under two weeks to start seeing the benefits. This is enough time to develop a good habit of changing the diet plan.

How to Cope When You're a Dairy Lover, but For Health Reasons You Must Go Dairy Free

There are some good diary food substitutes out there to help ease into a dairy free diet. If you enjoy your glass of milk, or milk on your cereal, you can use milk made from almonds, hemp seeds, oats, rice, or soy. These versions of milk come in calcium fortified so you can pour it over your bowl of cereal or use in your recipes to know you are receiving the dietary calcium your body needs.

Cheese is another big issue for dairy lovers. Cheese substitutes do a nice job in helping to continue to eat the foods you love. Rice and soy both make cheese substitutes. Care must be made when choosing a cheese substitute and choose those without any dairy ingredients. Some imitation cheeses may contain casein, which is derived from milk as a milk protein. Another option for cheese is the varieties made from goat or sheep milk.

Butter lovers can find relief from dairy in the form of margarine, which is butter-like spreads made from oils.

Yogurts are made from rice and soy too and normally are found in health food stores. They come in plain and fruit. You can also create your own flavor with the plain rice or soy yogurts.

Dairy free ice cream does a great job at replacing the ice cream cravings. The same milk substitutes are made into delicious dairy-free ice creams. Other ice cream alternatives are sherbets because these are not made from milk products. If you have access to a good health food store you can find the milk substitute products including sour creams and all sorts of imitation cheeses.

Go ahead and make pizzas and ice cream, just use the dairy substitutes. Knowing the foods that sneak in dairy ingredients helps to remain dairy free too. Aside from the obvious milk, cheese, ice cream, yogurt, and butter avoid these foods: chocolate (read the ingredients), dips, whey powder, mayonnaise, coffee creamer (even the non-dairy contains casein milk protein), canned cream soups, cold cut lunch meats (look for turkey or chicken that contains no additives or preservatives).

These are ingredients that may sneak into foods, so watch out for: lactic acid, lactate, lactalbumin, lactoglobulin, casein, caseinate, galactose, acidophilus milk, ghee, curds, nougat, potassium caseinate, sodium caseinate, malted milk, rennet, and whey.

Eating out at restaurants can be a challenge when it comes to a dairy free diet. Avoid Mexican and Italian, which each contains dishes riddled with dairy foods. Choose Oriental foods instead. Vegan restaurants that are dairy free. If eating at a general restaurant choose meals made of grilled meats, steamed vegetables, fresh fruits and always ask for them to leave the butter and cheese off. A salad bar will allow control over the meal choosing a vinegar dressing.

Dairy free cookbooks such as this one will help to come up with recipes and ideas for foods to cook. If you are dairy free due to cow's milk issues, ask about trying goat or sheep milk and milk products too. Many regular grocers carry goat's milk and goat's milk cheeses.

Even Children Will Love These Recipes

Having a child with dairy allergies makes it difficult at times for them to have the foods they love. The recipes in this cookbook are ones kids will enjoy and some are even fun to make and eat. Included are recipes for different flavored pancakes, hot cocoa, mac and cheese, turkey burgers, and a whole section on desserts and snacks. Children will love the yellow cake, the chocolate pudding, the fudge, the crunchy oatmeal cookies and more.

Dairy Free Food List

In order to have a comprehensive list of true dairy free foods you need to read the ingredients on every package and refer to the list of diary-foods above for reference. Generally, the obvious foods are meats, vegetables, fruits, nuts, and grains. Any dairy-free milk substitute product made from rice or soy to substitute for milk, ice cream, and yogurt. Margarines made from oils.

Sample 5 Day Dairy Free Diet Plan

An asterisk* indicates the recipe is included in this book. The snacks are to be eaten between the meals and for dessert after supper. In addition to the "2" snacks listed, include nuts, raw vegetables and fruit mixed in with the foods. This is a sampling of meals using some of the recipes in this dairy free diet recipe book. Feel free to add extra vegetables and fruits to the meals.

Day 1-

Breakfast - Buckwheat Walnut Muffins*, eggs, sausage (turkey, soy or pork), juice.

Lunch - Pork Barbecue Sandwiches*, French fries, Coleslaw*, beverage (tea or water or juice)

Supper - Tuna Casserole*, salad with vinaigrette dressing, beverage (tea, water or juice)

Snacks - Apple Crumb Dessert*, Fudge*

Day 2-

Breakfast - Milk Free Latte*, Orange Banana Berry Pancakes*, bacon (turkey or soy)

Lunch - Chicken and Fruit Salad*, beverage (water, tea or juice)

Supper - Salisbury Steak*, Mac and Cheese*, baked potato with margarine, salad with vinegarette dressing, beverage (tea, water or juice)

Snacks - Yellow Cake*, Crunchy Oatmeal Cookies*

Day 3-

Breakfast - Hot Cocoa*, Crepes*, bacon (turkey, soy or pork), orange slices

Lunch - Clam Chowder*, salad with vinegarette dressing, beverage (water, tea or juice)

Supper - Chicken Tortilla Soup, salad with vinegarette dressing, beverage (tea, water or juice)

Snacks - Coconut Flavored Rice Pudding*, Cheese Popcorn*

Day 4-

Breakfast - Banbergo Smoothie*, Basic Pancakes*, sausage (turkey, soy or pork)

Lunch - Chicken Noodle Soup*, salad with vinegarette dressing, saltine crackers, beverage (water, tea or juice)

Supper - Beefy Cabbage Casserole*, beverage (tea, water or juice)

Snacks - Chocolate Pudding*, Banana Coconut Honey Oat Bars*

Day 5-

Breakfast - Breakfast Banana Smoothie*, Granola Bars*

Lunch - Super Easy Vegetable Beef Soup*, salad with vinegarette dressing, saltine crackers, beverage (water, tea or juice)

Supper - Grilled Garlic Shrimp*, Coleslaw*, Cream Corn*, steamed vegetables, beverage (tea, water or juice)

Snacks - Pumpkin Pie*, Chocolate Rice Crispy Bars*

Kids Can Enjoy Dairy Free Diet Too

Thanks to soy, rice, and almond milk, kids will still get their yummy frozen treats. Make homemade dairy free ice creams, flavor it with fruits and nuts. Since there exists substitutes for all the dairy foods, kids will not have to feel like they are doing without their favorite meals. Make pizzas and cheeseburgers with cheese substitutes. Most recipes are okay if you substitute the milk ingredient with soy or rice milk. Just make sure to read through the recipe and see if they list any warnings about it.

Recipes:

Dairy Free Breakfast Recipes

Applesauce

Makes 4 servings

Ingredients:

*3 cups of apples (chopped, no peels and no core)
*3/4 cup of water
*1/4 cup of sugar (granulated)
*1/2 teaspoon of cinnamon (ground)

Directions:

Pour the 3 cups of apples into a saucepan turn heat to medium. Add the 2/3 cup of water, 1/4 cup of granulated sugar and 1/2 teaspoon of ground cinnamon. Place lid on pan and cook for about 20 minutes. Apples are done when they are soft, easily pierced with a fork. Remove from heat and cool to room temperature. Place apples and liquid in a blender and blend until smooth. Or mash with a fork or a potato masher until the chunks are gone.

Buckwheat Walnut Muffins

Makes 8 servings.

Ingredients:

*3/4 cups of buckwheat flour
1 1/2 cups of apples (finely chopped or grated)
*1/4 cup of flax seeds (ground)
*1/2 cup of almond milk
*1/2 cup of walnuts (chopped)
*1 egg
*3 tablespoons of coconut oil
*2 tablespoons of dairy free margarine
*1 tablespoon of honey
*1 teaspoon of baking powder
*1 teaspoon of cinnamon (ground)
*1/4 teaspoon of salt

Directions:

Preheat oven to 350 degrees Fahrenheit. Grease 8 cups in a dozen cup muffin pan.

In a large bowl add the 3/4 cup of buckwheat flour, 1/4 cup of ground flax seeds, 1 teaspoon of baking powder, 1 teaspoon of ground cinnamon and 1/4 teaspoon of salt and mix. In a different bowl add the egg and beat. Stir in the 1 1/2 cups of grated apples, 1/2 cup of almond milk, and 3 tablespoons of coconut oil. Do not over stir. Mix in the dry ingredients, careful not to over stir again. Fold in the 1/2 cup of walnuts. Spoon the batter evenly into the 8 cups and bake for 25 minutes until golden brown. Muffins are done with inserted toothpick in the middle comes out clean. Mix softened 2 tablespoons of margarine with the 1 tablespoon of honey and spread over the top of the muffins.

Pumpkin Spice Muffins

Makes 10 servings.

Ingredients:

*2 cups of whole wheat flour
*1 can of pumpkin (15 oz)
*1/2 cup of sugar (granulated)
*1/2 cup of raisins
*1/2 cup of water
*1 tablespoon of baking powder
*1/2 teaspoon of baking soda
*1/2 teaspoon of salt
*1/2 teaspoon of cinnamon (ground)
*1/4 teaspoon of nutmeg (ground)

Directions:

Preheat oven to 375 degrees. Spray 10 muffin cups with cooking spray and set aside. In a bowl mix the 2 cups of flour with the 1/2 cup of granulated sugar, 1 tablespoon of baking powder, 1/2 teaspoon of baking soda, 1/2 teaspoon of salt, 1/2 teaspoon of ground cinnamon, and the 1/4 teaspoon of ground nutmeg. Stir in the can of pumpkin, 1/2 cup of water, and the 1/2 cup of raisins. Spoon into the 10 muffin cups. Bake for half an hour or until the tops turn golden brown and are springy. Cool for 5 minutes, then serve warm.

Milk Free Latte

Makes 2 servings.

Ingredients:

*1 1/4 cups of rice milk (plain)
*3 teaspoons of instant coffee
*2 teaspoons of sugar (granulated)

Add the 1 1/4 cups of rice milk, 3 teaspoons of instant coffee, and 2 teaspoons of granulated sugar in a saucepan and turn heat to medium. Stir constantly and remove when liquid steams. Pour into 2 cups and enjoy.

Banana Nut Bread

Makes 6 to 8 servings.

Ingredients:

*1 1/2 cup of flour (all-purpose)
*1 cup of sugar (granulated)
*1/2 cup of canola oil
*1/4 cup of walnuts (finely chopped)
*3 bananas (ripe and mashed)
*1 egg
*1 teaspoon of baking soda
*1/4 teaspoon of salt

Directions:

Preheat oven to 325 degrees Fahrenheit. Spray loaf pan with oil/flour cooking spray. In a bowl, mix the 1 cup of sugar with the 1/2 cup of canola oil. Beat the egg first, and then stir in the batter. Add the 1 1/2 cups of all-purpose flour, 1 teaspoon of baking soda and 1 teaspoon of salt. Fold in the 3 mashed bananas and the 1/4 cup of finely chopped walnuts. Pour batter into the greased loaf pan and bake until toothpick inserted in the middle comes out clean, for about 60 minutes.

Basic Pancakes

Makes 6 servings.

Ingredients:

*2 cups of water
*1 cup of rice flour
*1/3 cup of potato starch
*2 eggs
*3 tablespoons of tapioca flour
*3 tablespoons of canola oil
*1 tablespoon of brown sugar
*1 1/2 teaspoons of baking powder
*1/2 teaspoon of baking soda
*1/2 teaspoon of salt
*1/2 teaspoon of guar gum
*margarine
*syrup

Directions:

Mix the 1 cup of rice flour, 1/3 cup of potato starch, 3 tablespoons of tapioca flour, 1 tablespoon of brown sugar, 1 1/2 teaspoons of baking powder, 1/2 teaspoon of baking soda, 1/2 teaspoon of salt and the 1/2 teaspoon of guar gum together in a bowl. Beat the 2 eggs and stir into the dry ingredients along with the 2 cups of water and 3 tablespoons of canola oil. Spray with cooking spray a griddle or a flat skillet or pan and warm to medium high heat. Spoon about 1/4 cup of batter onto the hot griddle or pan and cook until the middle bubbles and the bottom turns a golden brown, about 4 minutes. Carefully flip and cook until golden brown, 2 to 3 minutes. Add a pat of margarine and drizzle with syrup, serve immediately.

Orange Banana Berry Pancakes

Makes 4 servings.

Ingredients:

*1 cup of oat flour
*1 cup of rice milk
*1 cup of blueberries
*3/4 cup of orange juice (pulp free is best)
*2/3 cup of whole wheat flour
*10 strawberries (mashed)
*1 banana (mashed)
*1 tablespoon of baking powder
*1 tablespoon of sugar (granulated)
*1/4 teaspoon of salt

Directions:

In a bowl mix the 1 cup of oat flour, 2/3 cup of whole wheat flour, 1 tablespoon of baking powder, 1 tablespoon of granulated sugar and 1/4 teaspoon of salt and set aside. In a separate bowl, mix the strawberries and banana together until smooth. Fold in the 1 cup of blueberries and then add the 1 cup of rice milk, and the 3/4 cup of pulp free orange juice, stir until blended. Gently fold the dry ingredients into the fruit batter, stirring until blended. If the batter is too thick, add a little more rice milk. Allow the batter to sit for a few minutes while preheating the griddle or a flat pan to around 350 degrees Fahrenheit or medium high. If needed lightly spray the pan or griddle with cooking spray. Pour about 1/4 cup of batter onto the hot pan or griddle. Cook until the bottom begins to brown, the top will produce bubbles, takes about 5 minutes. Flip over and cook until bottom is golden brown, about 3 minutes. Add a pat of margarine and serve immediately with pancake syrup.

Breaded Pancakes

Makes 8 servings.

Ingredients:

*3/4 cup of breadcrumbs
*3/4 cup of soymilk
*1/4 cup of whole wheat flour
*2 eggs
*1 tablespoon of canola oil
*2 teaspoons of baking powder
*1/4 teaspoon of salt

Directions:

Put the 3/4 cup of breadcrumbs in a bowl and cover with the 3/4 cup of soymilk and the 1 tablespoon of canola oil. Meanwhile in a separate bowl mix the 1/4 cup of flour, 2 teaspoons of baking powder and 1/4 teaspoon of salt together. Beat the 2 eggs and add to the flour mixture. Stir in the breadcrumbs and milk. Spoon 1/4 cup of breadcrumb batter onto a hot griddle or skillet that was sprayed with cooking spray. Cook until bottom is golden brown, flip and cook until bottom is golden brown. Serve immediately.

NOTE: Good served with a pat of margarine and a sprinkling of powdered sugar or a drizzle of maple-flavored syrup.

Crepes

Makes 4 servings.

Ingredients:

*1 cup of rice flour
*1/2 cup of coconut milk
*1/4 cup of water
*2 tablespoons of cornstarch
*1/2 teaspoon of sugar (granulated)
*1/2 teaspoon of salt

Directions:

Add the 1 cup of rice flour, 2 tablespoons of cornstarch, 1/2 teaspoon of granulated sugar, and 1/2 teaspoon of salt to a bowl and stir. Add in the 1/2 cup of coconut milk and the 1/4 cup of water and stir. Heat a griddle or large skillet sprayed with cooking spray to medium high heat. Spoon 1/4 cup of the crepe batter onto the hot pan and cook until the edges start to brown and curl. Flip and cook until golden brown. Serve with favorite syrup or fruits.

Hot Cocoa

Makes 4 servings.

Ingredients:

*4 cups of soymilk
*8 tablespoons of sugar (granulated)
*3 tablespoons of cocoa (unsweetened powder)
*1 teaspoon of vanilla extract

Directions:

In a large saucepan, add the 4 cups of soymilk and turn heat to medium high. Stir in the 8 tablespoons of granulated sugar and 3 tablespoons of unsweetened cocoa powder, and 1 teaspoon of vanilla extract. Stir constantly until the cocoa becomes steamy. Serve immediately in mugs.

NOTE: For an added treat, add a peppermint stick in each mug.

Granola Bars

Makes 16 servings.

Ingredients:

*1 3/4 cups of oats (rolled)
*1 cup of crisp rice cereal
*3/4 cup of brown sugar
*3/4 cup of rice flour
*1/2 cup of walnuts or peanuts or almonds (chopped)
*1/2 cup of semisweet chocolate chips
*1/3 cup of margarine (softened)
*2 tablespoons of honey
*1 egg
*1 teaspoon of guar gum
*1 teaspoon of vanilla extract
*1 teaspoon of baking soda
*1/4 teaspoon of salt

Directions:

Preheat the oven to 350 degrees Fahrenheit. Spray a 9x13 pan with cooking spray. Add the 3/4 cup of brown sugar in a bowl with the 1/3 cup of margarine, cream together. Beat the egg, add to the batter, and stir in the 2 tablespoons of honey and 1 teaspoon of vanilla extract. Mix until creamy smooth. In a separate bowl add the 3/4 cup of rice flour, 1 teaspoon of guar gum, 1 teaspoon of baking soda and 1/4 teaspoon of salt. Gradually add to the batter, stirring well. Fold in the 1 3/4 cups of rolled oats, 1 cup of crisp rice cereal, 1/2 cup of chopped nuts, and 1/2 cup of semisweet chocolate chips. Spoon the mixture into the sprayed 9x13 pan. Pat down and bake until golden brown, about 20 minutes. Cool and cut into squares and serve.

Banbergo Smoothie

Makes 6 servings.

Ingredients:

*2 bananas (ripe, peeled, chopped and frozen)
*2 mangoes (frozen, peeled and chopped)
*2 cup of orange juice
*2 cups of strawberries (chopped)
*2 tablespoons of honey
*1 tablespoon of lemon juice

Directions:

Add the 2 cups of chopped strawberries to a blender and blend. Add in the 2 chopped frozen bananas and the 2 frozen chopped mangoes and "chop and blend" in the blender until smooth. Add in the 2 cups of orange juice, 2 tablespoons of honey and 1 tablespoon of lemon juice and blend for a couple of minutes until the texture is nice and smooth. Pour into 6 glasses and serve immediately.

Banana Blueberry Smoothie

Makes 4 servings.

Ingredients:

*4 cups of soymilk
*3 cups of blueberries
*4 ripe bananas
*1/2 cup of soy protein powder
*4 tablespoons of flax seed meal

Directions:

Put the 4 cups of soymilk and 3 cups of blueberries in a blender followed by the 4 ripe bananas (cut them into large chunks), 1/2 cup of soy protein powder and 4 tablespoons of flax seed meal. Blend until all ingredients are smooth. Serve immediately. If you wish, you may add a drizzle of honey to the mixture for extra sweetness.

Breakfast Banana Smoothie

Makes 4 servings.

Ingredients:

*2 ripe bananas
*3 cups of water
*1 cups of ice

Directions:

Add the bananas along with 3 cups of water and 1 cup of ice to a blender. Blend until smooth. Serve immediately.

Make a strawberry banana smoothie by adding a few ripe strawberries. Sweeten with honey if desired.

Lunch and Supper Recipes

Pork (or Lamb) Barbecue Sandwiches

Makes 6 servings.

*1 1/2 pounds of pork (or better -- lamb) ribs (deboned)
*1 1/8 cups of barbecue sauce
*1 cup of beef broth

Directions:

Add the 1 1/2 pounds of boneless pork ribs and the 1 cup of beef broth into a Crockpot. Cook for 3 to 4 hours on high, until meat is tender and easily shreds with a fork. Shred pork with forks. Place the shredded pork into a baking dish and cover with the 1 1/8 cups of barbecue sauce and cook in 350 degrees Fahrenheit oven for half an hour.

Serve on dairy-free buns or bread.

Chicken and Fruit Salad

Makes 6 servings.

Ingredients:

*1 pound of chicken breasts (skinless and boneless)
*2 heads of iceberg lettuce (washed, dried and torn into bite sized pieces)
*1 cup of strawberries
*1 cup of canola oil
*1/2 cup of pecans
*1/2 cup of sugar (granulated)
*1/3 cup of red wine vinegar
*1/2 onion (minced)
*1 teaspoon of mustard (ground)
*1 teaspoon of salt
*1/4 teaspoon of black pepper

Directions:

Prepare the grill for cooking the chicken. If no grill cook on the top rack of the oven under the broiler with a cookie sheet underneath to catch the drippings. Spray the grill with cooking spray, or lightly spray the chicken if cooking in the oven under the broiler. Cook about 7 or 8 minutes, making sure it is cooked to the center and the juices are running clear. Remove from grill or boiler and let cool a few minutes. Slice into strips. Heat a dry skillet to medium high heat and add the pecans for about 8 minutes, stirring often, and turning. Take off heat and place in bowl. Add the 1 cup of canola oil, 1/2 cup of granulated sugar, 1/3 cup of red wine vinegar, 1/2 minced onion, 1 teaspoon of ground mustard, 1 teaspoon of salt and 1/4 teaspoon of black pepper to a blender and blend until smooth. Divide the lettuce among 6 plates; divide the grilled chicken strips on top of the lettuce, as well as the cup of strawberries and half cup of toasted pecans. Pour the dressing over the top and serve immediately.

Clam Chowder

Makes 6 servings.

Ingredients:

*4 cups of potatoes (peeled and diced - russet or baking)
*3 cups of rice milk
*2 cups of clam broth
*2 cans of minced clams (6.5 oz)
*2 carrots (peeled and sliced)
*1 onion (diced)
*1 bay leaf
*1/2 cup of flour (all purpose)
*1 tablespoon olive oil
*1 tablespoon of parsley (dried)
*3/4 teaspoon of salt
*1/2 teaspoon of thyme (crushed)
*1/2 teaspoon of white pepper
*1/4 teaspoon of black pepper (ground)
*salt and pepper to season
*saltine crackers

Directions:

Pour the tablespoon of oil into a stockpot and heat on medium heat. Stir in the diced onion and the 2 sliced carrots. Stir and sauté until vegetables are soft. Add the flour, stirring for the roux, bust the clumps. Gradually add the 2 cups of clam broth, stirring until smooth. Stir in the 3 cups of rice milk. Add the 2 cans of minced clams along with the bay leaf, 1 tablespoon of dried parsley, 3/4 teaspoon of salt, 1/2 teaspoon crushed thyme, 1/2 teaspoon white pepper, and the 1/4 teaspoon of ground black pepper. Turn the temperature to high and bring to a boil while stirring often. Turn the heat down to simmer, put a lid on the pot, and simmer for half an hour. Add the 4 cups of diced potatoes and simmer another half an hour until soft. Remove bay leaf. Season with salt and pepper and serve with saltine crackers.

Chicken Noodle Soup

Makes 6 servings.

Ingredients:

*2 pounds of chicken (skinned, deboned and chopped)
*8 cups of water
*2 stalks of celery (chopped)
*1 onion (chopped)
*1 carrot (peeled and finely chopped)
*1 bay leaf
*6 ounces of noodles (flat egg noodles work well)
*1/4 cup of parsley (fresh chopped)
*1 tablespoon of salt
*1 teaspoon of seasoning (Mrs. Dash, Accent, or similar)
*1/2 teaspoon of basil
*1/4 teaspoon of black pepper (ground)

Directions:

Add the 8 cups of water to the Crockpot turned to high temperature and add the 2 pounds of chopped chicken, 2 chopped stalks of celery, 1 chopped onion, 1 peeled and finely chopped carrot, 1/4 cup of fresh chopped parsley, bay leaf, 1 tablespoon of salt, 1 teaspoon of seasoning, 1/2 teaspoon basil, and 1/4 teaspoon of ground black pepper. Cook for 5 hours and 30 minutes. Remove the bay leaf and add the 6 ounces of noodles and cook for 30 minutes. Add to soup tureen and cool slightly before serving.

Super Easy Vegetable Beef Soup

Makes 6 servings.

Ingredients:

*1 pound of ground beef
*1 can of tomatoes (28 oz - chopped)
*2 cans of beef broth (10.5 oz)
*1 can of green beans (16 oz)
*3 cups of potatoes (diced)
*2 cups of water
*1 cup of celery (chopped)
*1 cup of carrots (sliced)
*1 cup of onions (chopped)
*2 teaspoons of chili powder
*3 dashes of cayenne pepper sauce
*1 teaspoon of salt
*1 teaspoon of Worcestershire sauce

Directions:

Cook the pound of ground beef in a skillet, drain the fat and put the beef in a Crockpot. Add all the remaining ingredients and stir. Turn Crockpot to high for an hour, then on low for another 7 hours. Allow to cool slightly before serving.

NOTE: Add a few noodles during the last hour of cooking if desired. Add other vegetables like leftovers from the previous week too.

Cream of Chicken Soup

Makes 4 servings.

Ingredients:

*2 cups of chicken broth
*1/2 cup of chicken (cooked, finely chopped)
*2 potatoes (peeled and diced)
*1 carrot (peeled and thinly sliced)
*1/2 cup of celery (chopped)
*1/4 cup of celery leaves
*salt and pepper to season

Directions:

Pour the 2 cups of chicken broth into a pot and bring to a boil. Stir in the 2 diced potatoes, sliced carrot and the 1/2 cup of chopped celery with the 1/4 cup of celery leaves, bring to another boil. Put lid on pot and turn heat to simmer for 25 minutes. Allow to cool slightly, pour entire pot into a blender, and blend until smooth. Return to pot and add the 1/3 cup of cooked chicken and heat through. Serve warm.

Potato Soup

Makes 6 servings.

Ingredients:

*8 potatoes (peeled and diced)
*2 cups of chicken broth
*2 2/3 cups of water
*1 onion (chopped)
*7 slices of bacon (chopped)
*2/3 cup of bell pepper (chopped)
*2/3 cup of cheddar cheese substitute
*2/3 cup of rice milk
*4 tablespoons of green onions (finely sliced)
*2 tablespoons of margarine
*salt and pepper to season.

Add all ingredients to a Crockpot and cook on high for 4 hours or until the potatoes are softened. If desired, mash the potatoes with a potato masher. Season with salt and pepper.

Split Pea Soup

Makes 6 servings.

Ingredients:

*6 cups of chicken or vegetable broth
*1 package of split peas (16 oz. dried and rinsed)
*2 cups of ham (diced)
*1 1/2 cups of carrots (thinly sliced)
*1/2 cup of onions (chopped)
*2 stalks of celery (chopped with leaves)
*2 cloves of garlic (minced)
*1 bay leaf
*1/2 tablespoon of seasoning salt
*1/2 teaspoon of black pepper (ground)

Directions:

Pour the package of split peas into the bottom of a Crockpot. On top of that place the 2 cups of ham, 1 1/2 cups of thinly sliced carrots, 1/2 cup of chopped onion, 2 chopped stalks of celery and leaves and the bay leaf. Sprinkle on top of that the 1/2 tablespoon of seasoning salt and the 1/2 teaspoon of ground black pepper. Pour the 6 cups of broth over the top, no need to stir. Cook on high for 4 and a half hours, or until the peas are tender. OR cook over night on low for a total of at least 8 hours. Remove the bay leaf. Transfer to a soup tureen or large serving bowl to cool a little before serving.

Grilled Garlic Shrimp

Makes 6 servings.

Ingredients:

*2 pounds of shrimp (peeled and deveined)
*3 garlic cloves (minced)
*1/3 cup of olive oil
*1/4 cup of tomato sauce
*2 tablespoons of red wine vinegar
*2 tablespoons of basil (fresh chopped)
*1/2 teaspoon of salt
*1/4 teaspoon of cayenne pepper

Directions:

Add to a bowl the 3 minced garlic cloves, 1/3 cup of olive oil, 1/4 cup of tomato sauce and the 2 tablespoons of red wine vinegar and stir. Add the 2 tablespoons of fresh chopped basil, 1/2 teaspoon of salt and 1/4 teaspoon of cayenne pepper and stir. Add the 2 pounds of peeled deveined shrimp, tossing to coat. Cover the bowl and refrigerate for 45 minutes, tossing the shrimp every 15 minutes. Slightly oil a grill and heat to medium. Skewer the shrimp and cook for 3 minutes, then turn over and cook another 3 minutes. Do not reuse the marinade simply throw it away. Serve hot shrimp immediately.

Beefy Cabbage Casserole

Makes 6 servings.

Ingredients:

*1 1/2 pounds of lean ground beef
*1 cabbage (small size, shredded)
*1 can of tomato sauce (14 oz)
*1 cup of onions (finely chopped)
*1 cup of water
*1/2 cup of rice
*1 clove of garlic (minced)
*1 teaspoon of salt
*1/4 teaspoon of black pepper (ground)

Directions:

Brown the 1 1/2 pounds of lean ground beef in a skillet. Add the can of tomato sauce, 1 cup of finely chopped onions, 1 cup of water, 1 minced garlic clove, 1 teaspoon of salt and 1/4 teaspoon of ground black pepper and stir. Stir in the 1/2 cup of rice. Put a lid on and simmer until the rice is tender, about 20 minutes. Meanwhile preheat the oven to 350 degrees Fahrenheit. Spray a medium sized baking dish with cooking spray. Place half of the shredded cabbage on the bottom, cover with half of the beef mixture, add the remaining shredded cabbage and the remaining beef mixture. Cover with foil and bake for 60 minutes. All to cool for 10 minutes before serving.

Rack of Lamb

Makes 4 servings.

Ingredients:

*1 rack of lamb (7 bone trimmed, frenched)
*1/2 cup of bread crumbs (use fresh)
*2 tablespoons of garlic (minced)
*2 tablespoons of rosemary (fresh chopped)
*4 tablespoons of olive oil (divided)
*1 tablespoon of Dijon mustard
*2 teaspoons of salt (divided)
*1 1/4 teaspoon of black pepper (ground - divided)

Directions:

Preheat the oven to 450 degrees Fahrenheit. Pour the 1/2 cup of fresh bread crumbs into a bowl and toss in the 2 tablespoons of minced garlic cloves, 2 tablespoons of fresh chopped rosemary, 1 teaspoon of salt, and 1/4 teaspoon of ground black pepper. Drizzle 2 tablespoons of olive oil over the top and toss once more. Rub the remaining 1 teaspoon of salt and the teaspoon of ground black pepper on the rack of lamb. Heat the remaining 2 tablespoons of oil in a large skillet and brown the lamb, turning to all sides at least 2 minutes per side. Allow rack of lamb to cool for a couple of minutes, then rub the tablespoon of Dijon mustard over the lamb and then roll the rack of lamb in the bread crumbs, coating all sides evenly. Place foil on the ends of each bone. Place the rack of lamb in a baking dish or the skillet and place in oven for 18 minutes to well done. Remove from oven and allow cooling for about 6 minutes. Carve and serve.

Tuna Casserole

Makes 6 servings.

Ingredients:

*3 1/2 cups of brown rice pasta
*2 cans of tuna (6 oz packed in water)
*2 cups of chicken broth
*1 cup of mushrooms (sliced)
*3/4 cup of bread crumbs
*1/2 cup of peas (frozen)
*1/2 cup of onions (chopped)
*1/4 cup of olive oil mayonnaise
*1/4 cup of rice flour
*4 1/2 tablespoons of olive oil (divided)
*salt and pepper to season
*paprika to season

Directions:

Preheat the oven to 350 degrees Fahrenheit. Spray a 9x13 pan with cooking spray. In a skillet, add the 2 tablespoons of olive oil and heat to medium. Stir in the 1 cup of sliced mushrooms and 1/2 cup of chopped onions and sauté. Put onions and mushrooms in a bowl. Drizzle another 2 tablespoons of olive oil into the pan, heat up, and add the 1/4 cup of flour to make a roux, stirring with a whisk. Pour in the broth slowly, stirring constantly until it thickens into a bubbly gravy. Mix the 1/4 cup of olive oil mayonnaise and the salt and pepper in a cup, and then add the mixture to the gravy and stir. Drain the 2 cans of tuna and add to the gravy mixture along with the mushroom and onion mixture. Stir in the frozen peas. Place the 3 1/1 cups of brown rice pasta in the bottom of the baking dish, spreading evenly. Pour the gravy sauce over the pasta. Sprinkle the 3/4 cup of breadcrumbs over the top. Sprinkle the paprika over the breadcrumbs and then drizzle the remaining 1/2 tablespoon of olive oil over that. Bake until the top turns a golden brown, about half an hour.

Mango and Tuna Steaks

Makes 4 servings.

Ingredients:

*4 tuna steaks
* 1 mango (peeled, pitted, chopped)
*1 jalapeno pepper (seeded, minced)
*2 garlic cloves (minced)
*1 green onion (chopped)
*1/4 cup of red bell pepper (finely chopped)
*1/4 cup of onion (finely chopped)
*6 tablespoons and 1 1/2 teaspoons of olive oil (divided)
*4 tablespoons of lime juice (divided)
*2 tablespoons of paprika
*2 tablespoons of cilantro (fresh chopped)
*1 tablespoon of cayenne pepper
*1 tablespoon of onion powder
*1 tablespoon of garlic powder
*2 teaspoons of salt
*1 teaspoon of black pepper (ground)
*1 teaspoon of thyme (dried)
*1 teaspoon of basil (dried)
*1 teaspoon of oregano (dried)

Directions:

In a small bowl add the 2 tablespoons of olive oil with the 2 tablespoons of lime juice and the 2 cloves of minced garlic, whisking together and then put on the 4 tuna steaks, rubbing into the entire steaks. Wrap the tuna steaks tightly and refrigerate for several hours. In a separate bowl add the chopped mango with the minced jalapeno pepper, chopped green onion, 1/4 cup of finely chopped red bell pepper, 1/4 cup of finely chopped onion and the 2 tablespoons of fresh chopped cilantro. Pour the 2 tablespoons of lime juice along with 1 1/2 teaspoons of olive oil over and toss for even coating. Cover and refrigerate for an hour. In a large plate mix the 2 tablespoons of paprika with the 1 tablespoon of cayenne pepper, tablespoon of garlic powder, tablespoon of onion powder, 2 teaspoons of salt, teaspoon of ground black pepper, teaspoon of dried thyme, teaspoon of dried basil and the teaspoon of dried oregano. After the tuna steaks have been refrigerated for at least 3 hours, rinse them with water, and drag through the spices, both sides with all 4 steaks. Add 2 tablespoons of olive oil in a large skillet and turn to medium heat. Cook the tuna steaks for 3 minutes then add the remaining olive oil and cook the other side of the tuna steaks for 3 minutes. Divide the mango salsa among 4 plates, place a tuna steak on top of the mangos, and serve while still hot.

Chicken Tortilla Soup

Makes 8 servings.

Ingredients:

*1 pound of chicken (cooked, shredded)
*tortilla chips (normal sized bag)
*1 can of tomatoes (15 oz, peeled and mashed)
*1 can of chicken broth (14.5 oz)
*1 can of enchilada sauce (10 oz)
*1 package of corn (10 oz frozen)
*1 can of green chili peppers (4 oz)
*2 cups of water
*1 bay leaf
*2 garlic cloves (minced)
*1 tablespoon of cilantro (chopped)
*1 teaspoon of cumin
*1 teaspoon of chili powder
*1 teaspoon of salt
*1/4 teaspoon of black pepper (ground)

Directions:

Turn Crockpot to high setting; add the pound of cooked shredded chicken and pour in the can of tomatoes, can of chicken broth, can of enchilada sauce and stir. Add the package of frozen corn, can of green chili peppers (liquid and all), 2 cups of water, 2 minced garlic cloves, tablespoon of chopped cilantro, teaspoon of cumin, teaspoon of chili powder, teaspoon of salt and 1/4 teaspoon of ground black pepper and stir. Cook for 3 1/2 hours. Serve in bowls and crumble tortilla chips over the top.

Salisbury Steak

Makes 6 servings.

Ingredients:

*1 1/2 pounds of lean ground beef
*1 can of French onion soup (condensed 10.5 oz)
*1/2 cup of bread crumbs
*1/4 cup of ketchup
*1/4 cup of water
*1 egg
*1 tablespoon of Worcestershire sauce
*1 tablespoon of flour (all-purpose)
*1/2 teaspoon of mustard powder
*1/4 teaspoon of salt
*1/8 teaspoon of black pepper (ground)

Directions:

Put the 1 1/2 pounds of raw ground beef in a bowl and to it a third of the can of condensed French onion soup, the egg (slightly beaten), 1/2 cup of breadcrumbs, 1/4 teaspoon of salt, and 1/8 teaspoon of pepper. With bare hands (or gloved) squish together, and then create six patties. Place the patties in a skillet heated to medium high heat and cook until both sides are brown, about 5 or 6 minutes each side. Drain the fat from the skillet turn heat to medium low. In a bowl, add the tablespoon of all-purpose flour and the remaining 2/3 can of French onion soup. Whisk until smooth. Add the 1/4 cup of ketchup, tablespoon of Worcestershire sauce and 1/2 teaspoon of mustard powder and stir. Drizzle over the Salisbury steaks, put a lid on, and cook for about 20 minutes, stirring often.

Balsamic Vinegar Chicken

Makes 6 servings.

Ingredients:

*6 chicken breast halves (boneless and skinless)
*1 can of tomatoes (14.5 oz diced)
*1 cup of onion (sliced thin)
*1/2 cup of balsamic vinegar
*2 tablespoons of olive oil
*1 teaspoon of basil (dried)
*1 teaspoon of oregano (dried)
*1 teaspoon of rosemary (dried)
*1 teaspoon of garlic salt
*1/2 teaspoon of thyme (dried)
*black pepper to season

Directions:

Rub the teaspoon of garlic salt on the chicken breasts, sprinkle with black pepper. Add the 2 tablespoons of olive oil to a skillet and heat to medium. Add the rubbed chicken breasts and the cup of thinly sliced onions, sauté the onions. Add the can of tomatoes along with the 1/2 cup of balsamic vinegar over the chicken. Stir in the teaspoons of dried basil, dried oregano, dried rosemary, and dried thyme. Turn the heat to medium low and simmer the chicken until it is well done, when the juices are clear, about 15 to 20 minutes. Serve immediately.

Honey Rolled Chicken Kabobs

Makes 12 servings.

Ingredients:

*8 chicken breasts halves (boneless, skinless cut into bite sized chunks)
*2 1/2 cups of onions (cut into bite-sized chunks)
*2 red bell peppers (cut into bite sized chunks)
*1/3 cup of honey
*1/3 cup of soy sauce
*1/4 cup of canola oil
*2 garlic cloves (minced)
*1/4 teaspoon of black pepper (ground)

Directions:

Add the 1/3 cup of honey, 1/3 cup of soy sauce, 1/4 teaspoon of ground black pepper and 1/4 cup of olive oil in a large bowl, stirring. Dip out a ladle full and reserve in a cup for later use. Place the chicken into the marinade and put the 2 1/2 cups of cut up onions, 2 cut up red bell peppers on top, cover the bowl and refrigerate for 2 hours. (Overnight marinade soak is okay too.) Oil the grill and heat on high. Skewer the chicken, onions, and peppers. Brush with the reserved ladle of marinade during cooking.

Cook for 15 minutes on each side on the grill. Serve immediately.

Basic Fried Chicken

Makes 6 servings.

Ingredients:

*6 chicken breast halves (boneless, skinless)
*2 cups of canola oil
*1 cup of saltine crackers (finely crumbled)
*1 egg
*2 tablespoons of flour (all-purpose)
*2 tablespoons of potato flakes (from instant potatoes)
*1 teaspoon of seasoned salt
*1/2 teaspoon of black pepper (ground)

Directions:

Mix the cup of saltine cracker crumbs with the 2 tablespoons of all-purpose flour, 2 tablespoons of instant potato flakes, teaspoon of seasoned salt and 1/2 teaspoon of ground black pepper in a bowl. Beat the egg in another bowl. Heat the 2 cups of canola oil in a deep skillet or a deep-fryer on medium high heat or 350 degrees Fahrenheit. Drag the chicken breasts through the beaten egg, then coat with the cracker crumb coating by placing the crumb mixture in a gallon sized zipper bag and adding the chicken breasts, one at a time and shaking until well coated. Fry in the deep oil until well done, when the coating turns golden brown and the juices from the chicken runs clear. Serve immediately, can be store in the refrigerator and eaten cold too.

Coleslaw

Makes 8 servings.

Ingredients:

*1/2 cabbage (shredded)
*1 cup of carrots (shredded)
*4 tablespoons of raisins
*4 tablespoons of peanuts (toasted and salted)
*2 tablespoons of white wine vinegar
*2 tablespoons of apple cider vinegar
*2 tablespoons of green onions (thinly sliced)
*1/2 tablespoon of pumpkin seed oil
*1 teaspoon of brown sugar
*1/2 teaspoon of curry powder
*1/2 teaspoon of garlic powder
*pinch of chili peppers (ground)
*black pepper (ground - to season)

Directions:

Put the shredded cabbage in a serving bowl. In a separate smaller bowl, mix all the other ingredients together to form a dressing. Toss the dressing to coat the cabbage. Refrigerate for at least half an hour before serving. Store leftovers in the refrigerator.

Cream Corn

Makes 6 servings.

Ingredients:

*6 cups of corn (canned, frozen or husked)
*1 cup of onion (yellow, finely chopped)
*3/4 cup of chicken broth (divided)
*2 tablespoons of olive oil
*1 1/2 tablespoons of lime juice
*1 tablespoon of cilantro (fresh chopped)
*1 tablespoon of Serrano chili pepper (minced)
*salt and pepper to taste

Deseed the Serrano chili pepper before mincing. Add a cup of corn and half of the 3/4 cup of chicken broth to the blender and blend until smooth. Add the 2 tablespoons to a large frying pan and turn heat to medium. Sauté the cup of finely chopped yellow onion with a dash of salt. Pour in the remaining 5 cups of corn and sauté for a couple minutes more to heat through. Add more salt if desired. Pour in the corn and pepper puree mixture and simmer for 2 minutes. Pour in the remaining half of the chicken broth, the 1 1/2 tablespoons of lime juice and the tablespoon of cilantro and heat through. Add more salt and pepper to season.

Serve immediately.

Mac and Cheese

Makes 6 servings.

Ingredients:

*1 box of macaroni noodles (8oz)
*3/4 cup of liquid non-dairy coffee creamer (make sure it has no whey in it)
*3/4 cup of rice milk
*1 1/2 cups of cheddar cheese substitute
*3 tablespoons of margarine
*3 tablespoons of corn starch
*1 tablespoon of yeast (nutritional)
*1/4 teaspoon of black pepper (ground)
*1/4 teaspoon of paprika
*1/8 teaspoon of mustard powder

Directions:

Cook the macaroni according to the package directions. Drain the water and set aside. In a separate pan melt the 3 tablespoons of margarine and add the 3 tablespoons of corn starch to make a roux over low heat. Mix in the 3/4 cup of non-dairy coffee creamer and the 3/4 cup of rice milk. Whisk to make a white gravy sauce. Stir in the 1 1/2 cups of cheddar cheese substitute until melted and well blended. Stir in the tablespoon of yeast, 1/4 teaspoon of black pepper, 1/4 teaspoon of paprika, and the 1/8 teaspoon of mustard powder. Add the noodles and heat through. Serve hot.

Squash Soup

Makes 4 servings.

Ingredients:

*6 cups of butternut squash (peeled and diced)
*4 slices of bread (cut into bite sized chunks)
*4 cups of chicken broth
*1 cup of onions (chopped)
*1/2 cup of olive oil (divided)
*1 sweet potato (peeled and diced)
*4 garlic cloves (finely chopped)
*2 teaspoons of coriander (ground)
*1/4 teaspoon of salt
*1/4 teaspoon of black pepper (ground)

Directions:

Pour 1/4 cup of olive oil into a large saucepan and turn on medium heat. Sauté the 1 cup of chopped onions and the 3 finely chopped garlic cloves. Stir in the 6 cups of diced butternut squash, diced sweet potato, and the 2 teaspoons of coriander and sauté for 5 minutes. Pour in the 4 cups of chicken broth, turn heat to high, and bring to a boil. Turn the heat down to simmer until squash is soft for about 25 minutes, stirring occasionally. Pour entire contents into a blender or food processor and puree. Pour back into the saucepan and add the 1/4 teaspoon of salt and black pepper. Heat through. Meanwhile take the 4 slices of bread and cut into cubes. Heat 1/4 cup of olive oil in a skillet on medium, add the remaining minced garlic clove and the bread, and toss around while it "fries" for about 7 minutes. Remove from heat and serve with the soup.

Chicken A La King

Makes 4 servings.

Ingredients:

*2 chicken breasts (deboned, skinned)
*8 pearl onions
*1 1/2 cups of chicken broth
*1 cup of ham (cubed)
*1 cup of peas (frozen)
*1 cup of carrot (thinly sliced)
*3 sprigs of parsley
*2 celery leaves (from 2 stalks)
*1 bay leaf
*2 tablespoons of flour (all-purpose)
*2 tablespoons of margarine (melted)
*salt and pepper to taste

Directions:

Add the 2 chicken breasts to a large deep skillet along with the 1 1/2 cups of chicken broth, 3 sprigs of parsley, 2 celery leaves, and the bay leaf. Put a lid on and cook on medium low heat for about 20 minutes. Stir in the 8 pearl onions and the cup of thinly sliced carrots and cook another 10 minutes. Remove the chicken from the skillet and set on a plate to cool. Remove the parsley sprigs, celery leaves and the bay leaf, set aside. Cut the chicken into bite-sized chunks and add into the casserole along with the cups of ham and peas. Take 2 tablespoons of the broth and add to a cup. Whisk in the 2 tablespoons of all-purpose flour along with the melted 2 tablespoons of margarine. Pour the paste back into the broth in the skillet, heat on medium high for 3 minutes, stir constantly to avoid lumps. Pour the broth over the chicken, ham, and peas in the casserole dish.

Heat the casserole dish in the oven for chicken a la king at 400 degrees Fahrenheit for 10 minutes. Serve over rolls or toasted French bread. On the other hand, serve in a cooked piecrust for a chicken pot pie.

Lasagna

Makes 8 servings.

Ingredients:

*16 rice and corn lasagna sheets
*1 3/4 cups of ground beef (cooked)
*1 1/2 cups of rice milk (divided)
*1 zucchini (graded)
*1/2 cup of onion (chopped)
*1/2 cup of carrot (grated)
*2 sprigs of parsley (finely chopped)
*1 garlic clove (finely chopped)
*1 chicken bouillon cube
*1 bay leaf
*2 teaspoons of corn starch
*1 tablespoon of extra virgin olive oil
*1 tablespoon of quinoa grains
*1/4 teaspoon salt (+ more to season)
*3/4 cup of water
*breadcrumbs

Directions:

Brown the ground beef drain and set aside. Add the tablespoon of olive oil to a skillet and saute the grated zucchini, 1/2 cups of carrots and onions, chopped garlic clove and the tablespoon of quinoa grains. Stir in the cooked ground beef and the chopped parsley and heat through. Add the 3/4 cup of water with the bouillon cube and stir, cooking over medium heat for 20 minutes. Salt to taste. The mixture will be runny and this is okay. In a separate pan, heat the 1 1/4 cups of rice milk with the bay leaf. Once heated remove from the stove and discard the bay leaf. Add the 2 teaspoons of corn starch to the heated rice milk and heat again, stirring constantly until the sauce thickens. Take off heat as soon as it reaches a thick sauce consistency. Next layer the lasagna by spreading a couple of spoons of meat mixture in the bottom of a 9x13 baking dish, enough to "wet" the bottom. Place a layer of lasagna noodles followed by half of the meat mixture followed by half of the rice milk sauce. Then the last half of the meat sauce, followed by the lasagna noodles, and topped with the white rice milk sauce. Dust the top with breadcrumbs. Cover tightly with foil and cook in a 350 degree Fahrenheit oven for about 35 minutes, until the pasta sheets are al dente. Remove the foil for the last 5 minutes of cook time, then remove pan from oven and allow sitting for 10 minutes before serving.

Cabbage Soup

Makes 4 servings.

Ingredients:

*4 cups of vegetable stock
*2 heads of cabbage (shredded)
*1 tablespoon of soymilk
*white pepper to taste
*salt to taste

Directions:

Place the 2 heads of shredded cabbage in the 4 cups of vegetable stock in a sauce pan and bring to a boil and cook until the cabbage is tender. Salt and pepper to taste. Pour the soup into a food processor or blender and puree. Return to saucepan and add the tablespoon of soymilk, stir and heat through. Serve warm.

"Cheesy" Vegetable Casserole

Makes 8 servings.

Ingredients:

*1 pound of spinach (rinsed and chopped)
*1/2 pound of kale (rinsed and chopped, leaves only)
*1/2 pound of nettles (no thick stems)
*1 box of puff pastry (17.3 oz)
*3 potatoes (sliced and boiled)
*14 oz of mushrooms (white button)
*10 ounces of Monterey Jack cheese substitute
*1 1/4 cups of onion (chopped)
*1 cup of chicken broth
*3 eggs (divided)
*4 tablespoons of coconut oil (divided)
*4 garlic cloves (minced)
*1/8 teaspoon of liquid smoke
*salt and pepper to taste

Directions:

Allow the puff pastry to thaw outside of the package. Takes a little under an hour. Slice the 3 potatoes and boil until tender but not falling apart. Remove from heat and set aside. Heat the 3 tablespoons of coconut oil in a large skillet and add the 1 1/4 cups of onions along with the 4 minced garlic cloves and sauté. Gradually add the pound of chopped spinach, 1/2 pound of chopped kale and 1/2 pound of nettles, slowly stirring, and sautéing. Pour the cup of chicken broth into the greens and continue to cook until the greens are tender. Remove from heat, drain the chicken broth, and set aside. Shred the 10 ounces of imitation Monterey jack cheese and add the 2 eggs, beat slightly and set aside. If the puff pastry is thawed, roll it out and line a 9x9 baking pan, carefully patting down. Mix the cheese and eggs into the greens and place in the refrigerator. Preheat the oven to 350 degrees Fahrenheit. Add 1 tablespoon of coconut oil to a skillet and heat to sauté the 14 oz of white button mushrooms. Sprinkle in the 1/8 teaspoon of liquid smoke and mushrooms are done when they are softened. Add the mushrooms on the puffed pastry in the baking dish, then spoon the greens over the mushrooms, then add the potato slices. Season the potatoes with salt and pepper. Next, carefully place the puffed pastry over the top of the potatoes, carefully sliding the pastry inside the sides of the dish. Beat the third egg and brush the top of the pastry. Carefully set the baking dish on a cookie sheet and bake until the top is golden brown, about 40 minutes. Once done, remove and allow sitting for 10 minutes, then serve while still hot.

Sweet Potato Soup

Makes 8 servings.

Ingredients:

*1 large carton of beef broth (48 oz)
*1 pound of cremini mushrooms (finely chopped)
*5 potatoes (red grated)
*3 stalks of celery (diced)
*2 zucchinis (diced)
*2 leeks (sliced thin)
*1 sweet potato (diced)
*1/2 tablespoon of salt
*1/2 tablespoon of tarragon (dried)
*1/2 tablespoon of parsley (dried)
*1/2 teaspoon of black pepper (ground)

Directions:

Pour the 48 ounces of beef broth in a pot and bring to a boil. Add all the ingredients to the broth stir and simmer with a lid on for 60 minutes or when the vegetables are soft. Serve with bread or crackers.

Chicken and Dumplings

Makes 6 servings.

Ingredients:

*4 chicken breast halves (sliced)
*5 cups of chicken stock
*2 cups of cauliflower
*2 cups of broccoli
*2 cups of green beans
*1 1/3 cup of biscuit mix (make sure it is dairy-free)
*2 eggs
*1/2 teaspoon of corn starch
*water (about 1/3 cup)
*parsley (flat-leaf for garnish)
*salt and pepper to season

Directions:

Rub salt and pepper into the 4 chicken breasts and cook on the grill. Meanwhile pour the 5 cups of chicken stock into a large pot and add the 2 cups of cauliflower, broccoli, green beans and sliced chicken breasts. Bring the mixture to a boil. In a separate bowl add the 2 eggs and beat in the 1/2 teaspoon of corn starch with the 1 1/3 cup of biscuit mix. Add water until it makes a biscuit dough consistency, about 1/3 cup. Spoon the dough into the boiling broth and cook until the dumplings float to the top, for about 8 minutes. Serve immediately.

Turkey Burgers

Makes 4 servings.

Ingredients:

*1 pound of ground turkey
*4 slices of bacon
*4 whole wheat buns
*1/4 cup of onion (finely chopped)
*2 tablespoons of extra virgin olive oil
*2 tablespoons of parsley (flat-leaf chopped)
*4 teaspoons of olive oil mayonnaise
*2 teaspoons of poultry seasoning
*1 teaspoon of basil pesto
*1/2 teaspoon of paprika
*grill seasoning (to taste)
*lettuce
*tomatoes

Directions:

Cook the 4 slices of bacon. In a bowl, add the pound of ground turkey and mix with the 2 teaspoons of poultry seasoning, and 1/2 teaspoon of paprika. Mix in the chopped onions and form into 4 patties. Sprinkle the grill seasoning over each side and cook in a frying pan in the

2 tablespoons of extra virgin olive oil for 5 minutes each side. Meanwhile mix the 4 teaspoons of olive oil mayonnaise with the teaspoon of basil pesto and spread on each side of the bun. Put the cooked turkey patty on the bottom bun and break a slice of bacon in half and put 2 halves on each patty and top with a tomato slice and a lettuce leaf. Enjoy.

Snacks and Desserts

Banana Coconut Honey Oat Bars

Makes 9 servings.

Ingredients:

*1 1/4 cups of oats (regular oat meal)
*1 cup of bananas (mashed)
*1/2 cup of coconut (flakes)
*1/4 cup of flour (all purpose)
*1/4 cup of honey
*1 egg
*2 tablespoons of canola oil
*1 teaspoon of vanilla extract
*1/2 teaspoon of baking soda
*1/4 teaspoon of salt

Directions:

Preheat the oven to 350 degrees Fahrenheit. Spray an 8x8 baking dish with cooking spray. In a bowl, combine the 1 1/4 cups of oats with the 1/4 cup of honey, 2 tablespoons of canola oil and teaspoon of vanilla extract.

In a separate bowl, add the 1/4 cup of flour with the 1/2 teaspoon of baking soda and the 1/4 teaspoon of salt and mix. Slightly beat the egg and stir into the oat mixture along with the 1 cup of bananas and 1/2 cup of coconut flakes. Gradually stir in the flour mixture, careful not to over mix. Spread the thick batter into the sprayed 8x8 baking dish and cook until toothpick inserted in the middle comes out clean or about 28 minutes. Cool before serving. Store in the refrigerator.

Pumpkin Pie

Makes 6 to 8 servings.

Ingredients:

*1 pie shell (frozen kind or refrigerator)
*1 can of pumpkin (around 15 oz)
*1 cup of rice milk
*1/2 cup of brown sugar
*2 eggs
*1 1/2 teaspoons of cinnamon (ground)
*1/2 teaspoon of ginger (powdered)
*1/4 teaspoon of nutmeg (ground
*1/4 teaspoon of salt

Directions:

Preheat the oven to 350 degrees Fahrenheit and thaw the pie crust.

Beat the 2 eggs with an electric mixer, until frothy. Gradually add the 1/2 cup of brown sugar, 1 1/2 teaspoons of ground cinnamon, 1/2 teaspoon of powdered ginger, 1/4 teaspoon of salt and 1/4 teaspoon of ground nutmeg. Add the can of pumpkin and the cup of rice milk and beat until blended. Prick holes with a fork on the bottom. Pour the pumpkin batter into the uncooked pie shell. Place pie on a cookie sheet and bake for 45 minutes or until done (when the pumpkin pie filling is no longer runny. Cool before serving.

Cheese Popcorn

Makes 4 servings.

Ingredients:

*1/2 cup of popcorn kernels (unpopped)
*2 tablespoons of olive oil
*2 tablespoons of yeast (nutritional)
*1 tablespoon of margarine
*1 teaspoon of curry powder
*salt to season

Directions:

Het the 2 tablespoons of olive oil in a large pan or stockpot with a lid on medium high heat. Add the 1/2 cup of popcorn kernels and keep the lid on while shaking the pot over the burner until the popping stops. Put popped corn into a large bowl and drizzle melted margarine over it, then sprinkle the 2 tablespoons of nutritional yeast along with the teaspoon of curry powder and salt, toss popcorn to coat and enjoy.

Chocolate Pudding

Makes 4 servings.

Ingredients:

*1 1/2 cups of chocolate rice dream
*2 3/4 tablespoons of cornstarch
*2 1/4 tablespoons of brown sugar (packed)
*1 teaspoon of vanilla extract
*1/8 teaspoon of salt
*1/4 cup of semi-sweet chocolate chips

Directions:

Add the Rice Dream chocolate milk in a mid-sized saucepan along with the 2 3/4 tablespoons of cornstarch, 2 1/4 tablespoons of packed brown sugar, teaspoon of vanilla extract and 1/8 teaspoon of salt. Stir with a whisk or a fork. Turn heat to medium and stir continually as the liquid starts to boil. It will thicken a bit as it boils, turn heat off, and remove. Stir in the 1/4 cup of semi-sweet chocolate chips. Cool a few minutes, then spoon into 4 dessert bowls and serve. Store covered in the refrigerator.

Chocolate Rice Crispy Bars

Makes 12 servings.

Ingredients:

*2 cups of crisp rice cereal
*1 3/4 cups of coconut flakes (divided)
*3/4 cup of semi-sweet chocolate chips
*6 tablespoons of honey
*1/2 teaspoon of vanilla extract

Directions:

Grease an 8x8 baking dish with margarine. In a food processor, add 1 1/2 cups of coconut flakes and chop. Pour in the 6 tablespoons of honey and the 1/2 teaspoon of vanilla extract and blend for another half a minute to mix well. Pour the 2 cups of crisp rice cereal in a large bowl and mix in the remaining 1/4 cup of coconut flakes. Add the coconut, honey paste, and grease your hands with margarine. Then with your fingers incorporate the paste onto the cereal and coconut flakes. Put the sticky mixture into the 8x8 greased pan and press down evenly. Cover with foil and free for 10 to 15 minutes. Meanwhile put the 1/4 cup of semi-sweet chocolate chips into a microwave safe bowl and microwave for 1 minute, stir well. Remove the crisp bars from the freezer and cut into 9 squares. With your hands dip the bar to the half way point on the top of the flat side, then place on a sheet of waxed paper, chocolate side up to cool and dry.

NOTE: Add sugar sprinkles, chopped nuts, or more coconut to the top of the chocolate before it sets if desired.

Coconut Flavored Rice Pudding

Makes 6 servings.

Ingredients:

*2 cups of coconut milk
*2 cups of water
*1/2 cup of sugar (granulated)
*1/2 cup of basmati rice (rinsed)
*1 teaspoon of vanilla extract
*1 teaspoon of cinnamon (ground)

Directions:

In a saucepan, add the 2 cups of water along with the 1/2 cup of granulated sugar and the 1/2 cup of basmati rice. Turn the heat on high and bring the mixture to a boil, stirring occasionally. Once the liquid boils, reduce the heat to simmer and stir often for 20 minutes. Remove from heat and stir in the teaspoon of vanilla extract and teaspoon of ground cinnamon. Spoon into 6 dessert bowls and serve immediately. Store in the refrigerator and serve cold too, if desired.

Crunchy Oatmeal Cookies

Makes two dozen cookies.

Ingredients:

*2 cups of oats
*1 cup of trail mix
*2/3 cup of honey
*1/2 cup of flax-meal
*4 tablespoons of canola oil
*4 tablespoons of cornstarch
*1teaspoon of vanilla extract
*1 teaspoon of baking powder

Directions:

Preheat the oven to 350 degrees Fahrenheit. Using parchment paper, line a cookie sheet.

Add the 2.3 cup of honey with the 1/2 cup of flax-meal, 4 tablespoons of canola oil, 4 tablespoons of cornstarch, 1 teaspoon of vanilla extract, and the 1 teaspoon of baking powder. Stir to mix well. Fold in the 2 cups of oats and the 1 cup of trail mix. Grease your hands with margarine and shape into 24 balls and place a dozen at a time on the parchment paper on the cookie sheet. Bake for about 12 minutes, cookies are done when the edges turn golden brown, the top will have a slight sheen. Allow to cool before serving.

Yellow Cake

Makes 8 servings.

Ingredients:

*1 1/2 cups of flour (all-purpose)
*1 cup of soy milk
*1/2 cup of canola oil
*1 cup of sugar (granulated)
*1 tablespoon of vanilla extract
*1 tablespoon of vinegar
*1 teaspoon of baking soda
*1/2 teaspoon of salt

Preheat oven to 350 degrees Fahrenheit. Spray an 8 inch cake pan with cooking spray with oil and flour. In a bowl add the 1 1/2 cups of all-purpose flour along with the 1 cup of granulated sugar, teaspoon of baking soda and 1/2 teaspoon of salt. Stir to mix. Pour in the 1 cup of soy milk, 1/2 cup of canola oil, and the tablespoon of vanilla extract, using a whisk to blend into a smooth and creamy batter. Stir in the tablespoon of vinegar quickly and immediately pour into the prepared cake pan. Bake until a toothpick inserted in the middle comes out clean, about 30 minutes. Cool on a wire rack before removing from pan, serve, or frost and serve.

Fudge

Makes about 24 servings.

Ingredients:

*4 cups of confectioners' sugar
*1/2 cup of almond milk
*1/2 cup of cocoa powder (unsweetened)
*1/2 cup of semi-sweet chocolate chips
*2 tablespoons of margarine
*1 teaspoon of vanilla extract

Directions:

Mix together the 4 cups of confectioners' sugar with the 1/2 cup of cocoa powder. Add the 1/2 cup of semi-sweet chocolate chips. Pour the 1/2 cup of almond milk into a saucepan and turn heat to medium high, stirring constantly with a whisk. When the milk boils, turn heat off, remove saucepan from burner, and pour immediately into the sugar and cocoa mixture. Stir until all the chocolate chips melt. Grease an 8x8 pan with margarine and pour the fudge into the pan. Cover and refrigerate for a couple of hours. Cut into 24 squares.

Apple Crumb Dessert

Makes 6 servings.

Ingredients:

*6 apples
*1 1/2 cups of flour (self-rising)
*1/2 cup of almonds (sliced)
*1/2 cup of brown sugar
*1/2 cup of margarine
*1/2 cup of water
*1/4 cup of sugar (granulated)
*1 1/2 teaspoons of cinnamon

Directions:

Preheat the oven to 375 degrees Fahrenheit. Prepare the 6 apples by peeling and coring, then slice thin. Lay the apple slices in a pie pan and sprinkle with the 1/4 cup of granulated sugar and the 1 1/2 teaspoons of cinnamon. Pour the 1/2 cup of water over the top. In a bowl, add the 1 1/2 cups of self-rising flour with the 1/2 cup of almonds and 1/2 cup of brown sugar and mix. Stir in the 1/2 cup of margarine until it turns into "crumbs". Sprinkle the crumbs over the apples. Place on a cookie sheet in the oven and bake until the crumbs turn a golden brown about half an hour.

Dairy Free Diet Conclusion

Any diet plan needs the direction of your healthcare provider. While all of these recipes are dairy-free make sure to read the ingredients of the foods you use to make these recipes to be one hundred percent certain they are milk free. Always go over your diet plan with your healthcare provider, especially if you are eating dairy free for health reasons. These recipes should provide weeks worth of meals and snacks while avoiding dairy foods altogether.

www.ingramcontent.com/pod-product-compliance
Ingram Content Group UK Ltd.
Pitfield, Milton Keynes, MK11 3LW, UK
UKHW022225230426
12048UKWH00016BA/1075